Happy Birthd[...]
Enjoy
Love you
Bob & Jo

P9-EJU-370

p. 122

Other Books by Andrew H. Malcolm

Unknown America (1975)
The Canadians (1985)
Final Harvest: An American Tragedy (1986)
This Far and No More (1987)
Someday (1991)
U.S. 1: America's Original Main Street (1991)
The Land and People of Canada (1991)

HUDDLE

Fathers,
Sons,
and
Football

Andrew H. Malcolm

Simon & Schuster
New York London Toronto Sydney Tokyo Singapore

SIMON & SCHUSTER
Simon & Schuster Building
Rockefeller Center
1230 Avenue of the Americas
New York, New York 10020

SIMON & SCHUSTER and colophon are registered trademarks
of Simon & Schuster Inc.

Designed by Levavi & Levavi
Manufactured in the United States of America

1   3   5   7   9   10   8   6   4   2

Library of Congress Cataloging-in-Publication Data
Malcolm, Andrew H., date
Huddle: fathers, sons, and football/Andrew H. Malcolm.
p.   cm.
1. Malcolm, Andrew H.   2. Football players—United
States—Biography.   3. Journalists—United States—Biography.
4. Fathers and sons—United States.   I. Title.
GV939.M287A3   1992
796.332′092—dc20   92–10910
CIP
ISBN 0-671-76088-2

For Chris, Em, Spence, and Keddy
with appreciation for all their games—
past, present, and future—
and all the lessons we've learned together.

Acknowledgments

A book about football—or any such sport, really—must, above all, acknowledge the role of The Coach, one of the least understood, underappreciated, and probably most valuable positions in our society today.

Games reveal much about the values and character of a society. And the teacher of those games holds an extremely influential position. In my experience, coaches quickly become a surrogate parent-figure (and parents eventually become surrogate coaches). He or she simply stands there or paces just outside the athletic action, calmly or perhaps not so calmly, passing on the mechanics of strategy and the wisdom that comes from many games and encounters past. Coaches get all the blame for losses. On the other hand, they get none of the credit for victories.

My feelings about coaches are mixed. I have loved them for the time and interest they devoted to me; for their dedication to a job that involved me, improving me for a season or two; for the perspective and reservoirs of experience they shared with me. I especially loved them for how they made me feel by lavishing their wisdom on me. I have also hated them for all the uncomfortable, frightening, and even painful things, physical and mental, they made me do.

But I have always respected them.

Pick up a kitten by the back of its neck and the animal instinctively curls into a ball submissive to maternal authority. Say the word "coach" and to this day I automatically go into my respectful mode. Coach says this or Coach says that, like a nurse beatifying "Doctor."

The lives of many Americans may lack the traditional pair of parents these days. Even with two, they may be preoccupied with jobs and self. Sports become drop-off babysitters. In many cases coaches become substitute parents, at least for a few hours a day, with all that implies for the future. Although threatened by the equally modern reality of severe budget cuts, chances are at some point each of our lives is touched by a coach in school, Little League, or other youth sports. Over my formative years I probably spent more learning time with coaches than with any individual teacher.

That may seem superficially indicative of some skewed priorities in our society. But I don't believe so. Because my coaches were also teachers in the best sense of that tired old word. We didn't always have formal classes, and I didn't always realize what was happening at the moment. But standing there on the pressurized sidelines of athletic competition, the coaches were constantly imparting to me lessons that carried invaluable worth beyond the immediate game. Without really recognizing it until recently, I have been passing on those very same lessons as a parent-coach to my own youthful pupils.

For all those lessons and all that dedication and all those vibrant good times, I must thank all the coaches, on and off the athletic field, whose skills, insights, experience, dedication, and wisdom have so touched and enriched my life and the lives of everyone in my family.

Many of my coaches are gone now, physically anyway. For these coaches, I am sure, I was but part of a throng passing by in pads. But so generous were they with their experience, so intimate a part of my life were these individuals, so well did they seem to know what I was thinking and fearing, even when I didn't, that I know even now they can sense my appreciation from afar.

Many people have coached me over the years. I thank them all deeply. I want to acknowledge here those who did so athletically, especially Jock Sutherland, Chet Marshall, Arthur Hughes, and Ron Gleason, all at Culver Military Academy. They knew I could before I did.

I would also like to acknowledge the vital role of my ultimate coaches, my parents, Ralph and Beatrice Malcolm, who not only coached from the sidelines but put me in position and set me free to be coached by so many others.

My many teammates, who played such a major role in these stories, are too numerous to mention by name save for two special buddies. One of them is Dan Christman, better known to me as Bob for reasons of teenage emulation that still make sense. Ours was a friendship initially formed over Mom-made peanut butter and jelly sandwiches and then forever sealed within the bonds of football. I mention Dan here later.

The other special football friend is Doug Neumann, who isn't as dense as the spelling of his last name implies. One day after uncounted years apart we had agreed to meet on an airplane traveling to a mutual destination. A stewardess approached me. "Mr. Malcolm," she said, "Doug is waiting for you in the terminal."

I asked how she knew my name. "Well," she said, clearing her throat, "Doug said I should just look for the dumbest, red-haired son-of-a-bitch on the plane."

Those are the kinds of lasting friendships forged by enduring and enjoying the tensions, pains, and joys of intense athletic competitions together. The spirits become invisibly welded in some way so that, even years later, we pick up right where we left off. And we smile.

I also want to thank Ann Rittenberg and Paul Aron for having lunch that day when the seed for this book was planted.

I want to say how much I appreciate and admire all the many athletic and academic efforts of my children. Some of the early contests were a wee bit long, according to my personal index of Butt Boredom, but only until My Kids got into the game. Their dedication and participation have so enriched the life of this spectator that I cannot find adequate words. I so enjoyed being together with them then, even through sign language across the field. I hope they know anyway. As we approach the beginnings of T-ball with the next little Malcolm, I eagerly anticipate numerous Saturdays and Sundays once again in the *grand*-stands. Some people think these times concern "just games."

Above all, I want to thank Connie—my wife, my editing coach, and the best soccer coach in the family—whose suggestions and encouragements in the confusing marathon of creativity called writing a book have been, as always, insightful, invaluable, and, all right, I admit it, fun.

A.H.M.

Foreword

In my childhood, games were the most important thing in life. I lived to play them—hide-and-seek, tag, capture the flag, musical chairs, cowboys, and later, of course, spin the bottle. Living in the United States, the first team sport I played (not counting raiding kindergartners) was, naturally, baseball. That's what everyone did. Baseball was called the national sport then. Who was I to argue? So Dad and I went to many Cleveland Indians games, which was great fun. And I played baseball, too.

But for me, on its best days playing baseball was just okay. Everyone said it had a fantastically riveting strategy. So, of course, it must. Everyone said it was the all-American game. And I sure wanted to be all-American. But frankly, for me, watching baseball without Dad was right down there with watching cricket in the park by my great-uncle's house up in Canada. People arrived with great anticipation. The players were strong and lean and enthusiastic. They threw a white ball around with amazing accuracy. Sometimes they hit it. Then people ran all over. The spectators applauded. And I said to myself, Now what? What had I missed?

But that was all. Nothing came next. After a while everybody got up and went home and I felt that, if that was as colorful as fun got in life, then gray should be the national color. There had to be more to life than this game.

Any game is basically silly when you sit down and think about it. Imagine explaining golf to a visitor from an alien planet: Well, you put on red plaid slacks and a yellow shirt. You take a long stick. You get into position like a praying mantis, and you hit this little white ball across a large lawn. Sometimes it goes in the water and is lost, sometimes it gets mired in the sand, and sometimes it barely rolls into a little hole with a flag. Then you take it out of that little hole and do it seventeen more times.

Or soccer: Well, you run around on a field the size of Rhode Island kicking a spotted ball and butting it with your head, but not touching it with your hands. Every few hours someone kicks it into a net. Then everyone applauds or riots.

Or hunting: Well, you dress up like a soldier. You get a large gun. And you tramp around in the wet woods for hours hoping to scare a defenseless animal into running or flying away so you can shoot a large red hole in its unarmed side.

Or even fishing: Well, you sit in a boat holding a pole with a piece of string dangling in the water with a worm on the other end. If the moon is right and if it's raining really hard, then sometimes a creature down below eats the worm without telling you. Sometimes you catch it. The reward for such success is the opportunity to cut it open and clean it. The punishment is you've got to eat it.

The fact is that every sport has an attraction for someone (and I'm not referring to the multimillion-dollar salaries most of us won't get for playing). For me, football's initial attraction was simple: the legality of knocking people down. Such activity was prohibited at gym class and birthday parties. My father, the engineer, then suggested that there was more to football—to everything actually—than meets the eye. Dad said the same thing about baseball, to which my physical abilities did not lend themselves.

As a result, I fell in love with football. Toward that game I targeted all my hopes and ambitions, my dreams and struggles for several impressionable years. Having this passion also improved everything I did off the field, too. Football provided a ladder of achievement and a system of values at a time in my life when such accomplishment was crucial. I have carried that ladder and that system over into many aspects of my adult life. I continue to follow the game. I like its precision, its mental cunning, its physical bluntness, its spectacle, its unpredictability, its enduring and unforgiving values, its interlocking and ever-changing complexities, and especially the clarity of its decisive outcomes, which provide a relief from the overcast of incomplete outcomes that characterize so much of our daily lives. Football for me is like a living chess game that can't be adjourned or forfeited, no matter the score, no matter the weather. Even football's dangers, abuses, and outrageous characters provide lessons, little dramas that unfold on the sports pages like nonfiction Greek plays. Now, three decades away from playing my last football game, not a day goes by that I don't use several of the lessons I learned from football.

And, it seems, I am not alone. Football and football images pervade our society and are spreading now through a foreign professional football league. When the President of the United States leaves his desk at the White House, an aide always has in hand "the football," a black leather attaché case containing crucial documents and codes for any conceivable apocalyptic event. After the brief but successful war in the Persian Gulf in 1991, the American commander, sounding more like a coach than a general, commented, "When the kickoff came, our team was there to play."

Our language is full of football imagery. We tackle problems, block opponents, lob Hail Mary passes, strive for the goal line. If a situation is very bad, it's fourth down (third, if you're Canadian). What do we do if we're giving up? We punt, of course. Our wardrobe colors and shirts and the windows of our cars proclaim allegiance to favorite teams. Our recreation rooms are full of football-related paraphernalia. Our TV's produce countless commercials featuring football-playing or football-coaching spokesmen whose athletic acumen will surely pass on to us simply by buying that product and joining their team.

With more than two dozen professional teams and 2,061 games, our alleged national sport of baseball draws about 55 million spectators each year, an average of nearly 27,000 per game. With 28 National Football League teams and 224 regular season games, football has drawn 14 million paying customers each year, an average in excess of 62,000 per game. Of history's top ten most-watched television shows, fully half have been football games.

Individual readers will certainly draw their own conclusions as to what this augurs for the future. My professional journalism experience over a quarter century with *The New York Times* tells me to avoid grandiose generalizations. It seems safe to say, however, that a helluva lot of people like football. If that includes you, reading this book about football and how it has linked three generations of males in one family—mine—will, I hope, be an evocative journey through the feelings and sensations of a beloved and surprisingly complex pastime. Perhaps it will help you to understand just why you like it. For everyone else, I hope these experiences, these scenes and phrases, and the bonds these minute incidents in human history have provided for one family will help explain the power and the invisible attraction behind this amazingly popular phenomenon. Who knows? You might even come to enjoy it, too.

Andrew H. Malcolm
The Yaak, Montana
March 1992

HUDDLE

It started on a gray Saturday afternoon, one of those monochrome matinees where dusk seeps in unnoticed. I was sprawled on the living room rug, the bristly, rose-colored one with all the curlicue patterns designed to mask the appearance of any lint so stupid as to land in my mother's house. The rug had a scallop-shaped burn mark by the fireplace where an errant spark had landed in open defiance of her. Every time she entered the room, that mark had to suffer Mom's gaze, which may explain why the scar never healed.

Mom had already completed her first postlunch dust patrol, so I had the room to myself for a while. Actually, as the only child of two only children, I could almost always have any room to myself anytime. There were a lot of empty spaces in those days.

Although it was still early afternoon in our Cleveland duplex, several hours before television viewing was usually permissible, my mother had allowed me to turn on the tiny black-and-white set we had recently purchased, used. TV's were still new then—my grandfather would have called them newfangled. TV's were not yet the common-law spigots of information, shared emotion, free baby-sitting, and pervasive purveyor of implied values they would later become for a disparate nation with too much money and leisure time to spend. When the next nearby family bought their television, all the neighbors would troop through of an evening to see the device, to utter ardent admirations, and to retreat to their home in silent jealousy.

The picture on the twelve-inch screen of our Dumont was grainy. But the test pattern with the digital clock was gone that afternoon and in its place were some amazing moving pictures of something happening at that very moment about 150 miles away. Instantly seeing something far away was a powerful novelty in the early 1950s before we learned that everything is show biz with the genuineness and sincerity of a Broadway producer. I had, of course, seen two-day-old film of the ongoing Korean War: dark pictures of hollow-eyed dads interminably trudging along the sides of dirt roads in a faraway land that might as well have been the moon, although I had looked up Korea in the atlas.

So, watching something quite distant occurring at that very moment was in itself wondrous to my newly bespectacled, seven-year-old eyes, especially since the on-screen activities resembled war. This was some kind of game. It was happening at Ohio State University, which, although I had never seen the school, had earned my undying loyalty because of its physical location in my home state and because it wasn't Michigan.

Some very large students—they had to be students, right?—would gather on the field in a group, seemingly to talk. There were eleven on each side, if my whispered count had gotten everybody. A man in a striped shirt would rotate his arm while blowing a whistle and then stand by the plotting group. This was to eavesdrop, as best I could determine. The two teams would then confront each other across the white line. They paused for a moment. Sometimes a long moment. Then everyone tried to knock everyone else down. A whistle would blow. They would unpile, and do the same thing over again and again and again.

Once in a while, to break the monotony that was so obvious to me, one player would kick the ball high in the air while everyone tried to knock everyone down. Then the running around would resume with more knocking down.

Now, I liked knocking people down as much as any other second-grade boy who had spent his share of time, maybe more, awaiting execution outside the principal's office by the trophy case that could have used a quick dust by my mother. Watching this game was not quite as bad as a visit to the dentist's strange-smelling office downtown. But it was real close.

There were no bats to swing. No home runs to stroke. No bases to run. No dramatic slides to win the game. No brush tags in the nick of time. This game on television was pure adulterated boredom.

I considered myself a very serious fan of sports, which was the kind of simple news that seemed safest and easiest to follow at seven years of age. It still does. There was a winner and a loser every day, every game. No ties or "on the other hands" to muddy the waters of comprehension. There were good guys, who were the Cleveland Indians, and there were bad guys, who were everybody else.

I didn't know then that the word "fan" derived from "fanatic." But I was a very serious fan of the Cleveland Indians, and I had an Indians hat to prove it. That blue hat with the grinning Indian brave with the TV teeth went everywhere with me and looked it. If I didn't wear that hat everywhere, the Indians would lose. Which didn't help them in the '54 World Series but has certainly proven true since that betrayal. "You know," my frantic mother once said in another vain but, I must say, imaginative attempt to get that hat off my head for at least a few minutes every day, "if you wear a hat indoors, you'll go bald."

This theorem seemed eminently believable. Look at Jimmy Durante and Walter Winchell. Or Jimmy Dudley, the Indians announcer, who always wore a father-type fedora on the evening news. He didn't have a hair left on his body so far as I could see. But he didn't seem to be in a lot of pain for his baldness. In fact, he got to go to every single Indians game, which I had to watch on the radio and read about in the next day's newspaper. So the battered Indians hat stayed right where it belonged, on my red head, even at bedtime. Although by morning, the cap seemed to have somehow made its way over to the nearby chair. Which made it possible, come daylight, for that hat to go on even before the underpants.

I had collected every newspaper article and Teepee Topics trivia column about my Indians in a scrapbook that the Smithsonian would mortgage its soul for if it only knew. My father would sit down to read the evening newspaper, which is what fathers did in the evening in those days. He would pick up the sports section. And it would fall apart in his hands. Some pages had just a huge hole through the middle. The remnants of others were shaped like the letter U or L, possibly with some tape administered here and there. His lap would be littered with fragments. "I see," Dad would say to Mom, looking straight through what had been page C4, "that Andy brought the paper in today." I have now fallen about thirty-eight years behind in my newspaper clipping of Indians stories, which I blame on football.

I also collected every program from every Indians game my dad and I had attended together. The programs usually had some Municipal Stadium mustard on a corner. They were locked open to the box-score page, which Dad kept religiously up-to-date after each batter with precise penciled notations on that inning's events. ("Hey, look at that! Jim Hegan's first hit of the year." Probably his last, too.) Some programs would have had illegible autographs on their cover. Autographs were important in those days not because they might bring big bucks someday but as an excuse to actually exchange three words with titans like Early Wynn or Ray Narleski.

"Good luck, Early."

"Thanks, son."

"Wow! Did you hear that, Dad? He said, 'Thanks.' " I had made a link with fame.

Such an exchange enabled me to claim a measure of that afternoon's victory. But I must admit now before everyone that I did not keep the autographs from that morning in the Philadelphia hotel. Dad was checking in. The desk clerk told me that all those men lounging in the lobby chairs were baseball players. I had not known that they played baseball in Philadelphia. I ran off with pad and paper. All the old ladies sitting around would have found the scene awfully cute, the little guy in the blue baseball cap moving from leather chair to leather chair. "Hello, sir. May I have your autograph, please, sir?" (Politeness worked every time.) "Thank you very much, sir."

When I got back to the counter, I counted them up. There must have been *twenty* or more. Talk about striking it rich. It was great! But wait. I didn't recognize this name. Or that one. Or these down here. Or any of them really. Who were these guys anyway?

"Why, son," said the excited clerk, "they're the Pittsburgh Pirates."

"The who?"

They were the Pirates, from that famous ocean port of Pittsburgh? Wait a minute. If these Pirates were such a big deal, how come they never played the Indians? Or course, I knew other cities had baseball teams; they assembled in order to play my Indians. But other cities playing other cities? I had just spent ten minutes of my life accumulating the autographs of some nobodys who weren't even in the same league with the Indians. How mortifying! Just so

Jimmy Dudley never heard about it. I doubt if I got even one Bob Lemon card for the whole lot. So much for Philadelphia, which deserved Pittsburgh.

From this complete waste of time emerged Andy's Theory of Autograph Hunting: Always hang around the dugout so you can tell who these guys are anyway.

Appreciating sports, a youngster quickly learns, involves learning a lot of rituals as well as rules. Rituals are vital, often meaningless but absolutely vital. And learning them becomes an important part of the initiation into the sport. Watching 375-pound men toss some handfuls of salt around a dirt ring is boring to football fans. But to aficionados of sumo wrestling, it is an important part of purification. Some rituals are programmed—the coin toss, the handshakes. Some are very personal—the batter tapping his shoes with the baseball bat, me always putting on my left sock and football shoe first. In addition, before every game at the stadium, Dad and I went to the same restaurant, Jim's Steak House in downtown Cleveland. We went there many other times, too. But when it was decided that the two males in our family were going to "A Game," it was understood that this included a huge meal at Jim's. Also unstated but required was that I have the exact same meal every time: ground sirloin, no bun, with hash brown potatoes.

More than thirty years later, I found myself in a Cleveland motel room preparing my children to attend a game. One of them, naturally, inquired, "Are we going to eat first?"

I looked at him in shock. But of course, how could he know? Within the hour, we were sitting by the big picture windows of Jim's Steak House and the ground sirloins were cooking. We had to get to the stadium in time for batting practice, in case any foul balls came flying our way.

At the stadium with my father after the pregame warm-ups (Look, there's Jimmy Dudley with his hat), Dad and I would make our way up to "our" seats, which we allowed others to use if we were absent. Our seats were in the upper deck behind third base. This provided a better view into the Indians dugout so that I would know as soon as possible when Al Lopez was going to signal Don Mossi to start warming up. More importantly, however, that seat location was where it seemed most likely that a foul ball would plummet into my worn fielder's glove.

I sat there inning after inning, bolt upright, following every pitch, awaiting my lucky lightning strike. If it ever came my way, I would be quick off the bat, spearing the blessed ball before it soared into some thief's hands. My Indians cap was firmly in place. My right hand nervously pounded the glove on my left hand except, of course, when it was hot dog time. Which was to be, of course, precisely when "my" foul ball would come someday.

Dad kept score. And the way he watched the game, collected the secret signals from pot-bellied coaches, the way he stored all that game intelligence and described the patterns to me was truly impressive, as was most anything he said or did or signalled to me with his eyes or hands or voice, or even with the tilt of his head.

I don't know how it happens, but there was a moment early in the life of little boys in my generation—I imagine that it's late on a Saturday morning—when somehow even the most mundane mutterings of Dad became annointed as the Voice of God. What moms say are The Rules, or at least Her Rules. But what dads say is The Gospel. Most of the time these men don't even know when it happens themselves. One minute they are mere mortal men who blow their noses like everyone else; the next they are forever Dad, Voice of Experience, Judge Advocate, Platoon Leader, Chief Guy, Head Coach. This aura is enduring, waterproof, and resilient. It resists time and rust though not resentment. It will surround them for the rest of their life, even afterwards, it seems. They don't impose it or control it, though they can use it. This aura can rub off onto others at times. Coaches benefit from it. Generals, too. Later, even some astute bosses use it. But it starts with Dad and, typically, it involves sports.

I'm sure my dad knew a lot about cost projections, inventory accounting, and lots of other things from his daily work life that I never saw so couldn't appreciate. Judging from all the adding machines in his office, his work involved a lot of arithmetic. For me, the Dad Aura began to emerge around woodworking and then flowered around sports, a legacy no doubt of his rural prairie upbringing where you did for yourself or you did without. He could take a plain piece of wood and turn it into anything, as if he was molding it like clay: a lamp, a bowl, candlestick holders, a toy truck, a bed, a toy chest.

I learned the alphabet that way, one letter at a time, one letter each night. Standing at his basement workbench, he would help me trace the letter's outline on a piece of wood with a chewed pencil stub. Standing behind me, reaching over my shoulders, he would guide my hands guiding the saw. He would help me sand and buff the emerging character. My God, how we sanded and buffed that block of wood because, he said, "Anything worth doing is worth doing right." I would feel him there, guiding, watching. I still do. And here I am sanding and buffing those same letters into words about him and us.

So when one day Dad suggested that I watch the baseball game, really watch it, not idly watch it while awaiting my foul ball, there really seemed to be no choice in the matter. Dad says study this carefully, so you do. And then, over much time, the whole process of really examining becomes an ingrained thought pattern, a habit infused with verity beyond questioning.

"If you don't understand something," Dad said many times, "then take it apart with your eyes and mind. Watch one piece over and over. And another. And pretty soon you'll see how they work. Then you can fit everything back together."

This made perfect sense to my mustachioed father, the experienced engineer whose entire professional life was spent studying intricate industrial processes step by step, choreographing the best ones, and eliminating the inefficient ones. And so I, the sole heir apparent to this wealth of mental processes, had engraved that edict on my young mind like a biblical proverb. "Nevermind the ball," he'd say. "Just watch his feet, his hands, his eyes."

Now just exactly how the feet of Vic Wertz at first differed from Bobby Avila's at second as seen from the upper deck of Municipal Stadium was not readily apparent to me, although I did come to notice that each man had different assignments in different situations. Look at that. With a man on first, Wertz stayed closer to the bag and Bobby edged over more into the gap. The two of them didn't even talk about it. I hadn't noticed that. At first base, Wertz stood still, guarding it, even at the crack of the bat. Over at second, Bobby didn't seem to move so much as he flowed. He dove. He scooped. He jumped. He threw. He knew right what to do. And it wasn't always throw to first. He was a marvel. And look, when the ball was hit to the outfield, the infielders didn't just watch. They all moved into different places, prepared for the next steps that each member understood without talking.

I began to envision the flow, even at home listening on the radio. "Ground ball to short," Jimmy Dudley would say. Okay, Strickland's moving in front of it. The man on first is breaking for second. Bobby's moving over to cover there, his eyes alert, his glove ready. "Strickland takes it on one hop." Now, quick, get it to Bobby. "Tosses it to Avila." Yes, yes. Now, Bobby, quick, rifle it to first. "Avila's got it, throws to first." Yes, Vic, stretch, stretch. "Wertz reaches and heeeeee's— Got him!"

Yes, sir! This was amazing. Like a machine, only the parts were alive. If you paid attention and watched well enough, and thought quickly enough, you could almost know what was coming. Now, seeing into the future was something that grabbed me, like the idea of flying. There were an awful lot of pieces to learn in this sport. It was very tiring to keep track of everything—and always to remember to keep track. But I was beginning to unlock a very intriguing box here. This baseball was good. Very good.

Now before me on the TV screen on this Saturday afternoon was yet another baffling process. How many of these could there be in life? On this minuscule screen were people the size of peanuts running around as yet oblivious to the silent watching eyes that so far outnumbered those in actual attendance.

"It's football," my father said.

"It's boring," I said.

"Why?" he said.

Oh, no, here we go again. I had just blurted out the words without much thought. He could tell. He always could. He did not admire that. How could he always know what my thoughts weren't? Was there a dial somewhere on the back of my head that only Dad could see? And when the brain needle fell into the red "Dormant Zone," Dad would know to say, "Why?" And that would jump-start some actual mental activity.

"Well," I said, improvising quickly, "everything is so confused."

"To you," he said.

Yeah, well, that's who we're talking about here. "I just turned it on," I added hastily, hopefully. "I'm watching, uh, this player here."

"Uh-huh," he said. "Good choice. He's a guard. He'll tell you the play every time."

Oh, c'mon, Dad.

"This time the ball's going to theeee—right."

And it did. By golly, the ball went right where Dad predicted. I turned to look at him in amazement. He looked down at me with one of those "clever, eh?" smiles of his. "Wow," I said, but my face asked, "How?"

"Watch his feet," Dad whispered. There was no one nearby to overhear the secret, but that's what dads do to inspire close attention.

And so I ignored the ball. I watched the guard's feet. Sure enough. If he sought to push the defense to the left, the ball went to the right. If he blocked to the right, it went left. Okay, I got that.

But then, one time, the guard just stood there. That time, the ball was thrown. I filed that pattern away. Then, again he just stood there. Pass, I said to myself. But then, suddenly, the guard ran right. And the back followed. Ah, pretty tricky. This was getting to be kind of intriguing, not as good as baseball, of course. But football might help carry the scrapbook industry over until spring training.

And so I watched closely some more. And Dad, sitting behind, watched me watching them. And I felt it. After a while, my confidence grew. And I would make my own hasty play predictions. Standing still? "Pass!" And the guy with the ball must have heard me because in an instant there went the ball lofting through the air. And I turned to Dad, smiling, because I had broken the code. He nodded approval and that felt very good.

Our team didn't seem to pass much in those days. Dad said that was because we were Ohio State and Coach Hayes didn't like to pass for some reason. "Only three things can happen when you pass the ball," Dad said Coach Hayes said. "And two of them are bad."

This Hayes guy spoke like a minister, bafflingly. But okay. Hey, he was the boss, right?

At dinner, Mom asked, as women tend to do when they want to indicate interest and they think they've put their finger on the most important thing, "Who won?"

I was not sure. "We did," I said. "I think. I was watching the guard." This did not lead to prolonged conversation because, I now know, to her, guards were men who stood around banks watching for suspicious customers.

So, feeling charitable due to my newfound wisdom, I

shared another insight with her. "Ohio State doesn't pass much, Mom, because only two bad things can happen then."

Good thing she didn't ask what they were.

□   □   □

Dad had never played football, just rugby, but he drew a diagram for me of all the football positions so, if I wanted, I could study them one by one over those fall weekends. I definitely wanted. And on Saturdays, if Mom had not turned on the Metropolitan Opera on the large radio that dominated every living room in those days, then Dad and I would sit by the TV set together and have a kind of Socratic sports experience.

"Now," he'd say, "why do you suppose they passed this time and not on the last play?"

"To fool the defense" was my answer, although it came out with a question mark.

"Could be," he said. "Also, it was third down this time. So they were running out of downs, weren't they? And they still had seven yards to go. Have you seen them run that far yet today?"

"I don't think so."

"Right. So because they didn't get many yards on first and second down, they had to get it all on third. Kinda risky, huh?"

"Yeah. But wait. What if they passed on first down?"

"Tricky. That might work. But what if it didn't? Then you'd have to pass on second and third for sure and the defense would know that, wouldn't they?"

"How would the defense know that?"

"Because the defense watches where the ball is and how far it has to go."

"Boy, there's a lot to think about."

"Oh, look," Dad said. "Did you see the guard that time?"

"Well, yeah. He ran the wrong way, away from the ball."

"Why do you suppose he did that?"

"He's confused, too."

"Maybe," Dad suggested, "he was trying to fool the defender. See, the other guy followed him. The guard didn't even touch him. But he took him right out of the play so he couldn't make the tackle. Clever, huh? Like camouflage."

I had thought that if you weren't the star carrying the ball, then you were in the way. One star to score and ten guys for decoration. But every player had a different assignment every time. Each assignment varied according to the ball's position and the down and the quarter and the score. And the assignment could change depending on how the defensive player reacted or how the offensive player thought the defensive player would react, if he'd studied him closely enough. Like a catcher knowing a batter's weakness for curveballs down and in.

The sudden realization that football, like baseball and maybe a few other things in life, had intricate inner workings, no less vital for being hidden, was the dawn of a new age in my life. Only those informally initiated into the sport's appreciation could understand the intricate workings. And if they didn't believe in the intricate wonder of it all, then they'd never be able to understand it. I began to believe.

Sometimes every football player might mesh perfectly with all the others on his team in front of noisy thousands. The power of these unspoken links between humans was magnified by its silence. Eleven pieces suddenly fitting together in fleeting perfection. And being instantly rewarded. Eleven others stumbling and being promptly punished. Play after play, game after game, week after week. Always a new chance to win, to lose, to improve. Like life, only with justice. And without the grays.

"That's teamwork," Dad said.

The concept of teamwork seemed at first to threaten the sheer delight of imagining myself going out on the field and running around wildly all over the place making tackles and scoring touchdowns and receiving the crowd's adulation. I did not have to share Christmas with any other kids. No sharing on my birthday. Why should I share any of the glory that would surely come my way someday?

But the idea of so many different things going on at the same time while I sought to discern the hidden task of each man, sometimes enabling me to predict the future path of a particular play, was very exciting. And intriguing. Virtually every player was involved in virtually every play, not like baseball where eight-ninths of the batting team sat on a bench like spectators half the time. Football was my kind of mind game, where some people got knocked down and others did the knocking down and others cheered. And, for better or worse, by the end of the game, everything was resolved, unlike so many other things in the mess of life, such as long division with remainders.

And so I watched football some more. And Dad watched me watching it. And we were together then. Our own team. At home.

We still are.

☐ ☐ ☐

My mother did not like football. She never said so, but I knew, as little boys do when those secret signals seep out of their mother's pores. A lot of mothers don't like football. They see it as rude and crude, violent and baffling. Also, you might get hurt. As if anything—say, driving—is safe. Moms often go to the games, as mine did, because their son is playing. Because they think they should. But they just watch their boy's number and visibly wince a bit at each collision, seizing any excuse to talk about something else with another mother nearby.

My mother saw football the way some people see auto racing: She believed everyone went for the crashes. My parents and I did one sport together—once. We went bowling. Mom was a little awkward, or at least she thought people saw her that way. And then as I leaned over to let one surefire strike go right at the line, from my shirt pocket tumbled my Red Ryder BB-gun ammo pouch. On impact, it popped open and disgorged about twelve hundred little BB's all over our entire alley.

Even before the last little metal ball had stopped rolling down the long wooden alley, I had turned to my father. He stood there, frozen, quietly disbelieving. His style was not to blow up. He favored the Socratic stupidity approach, asking firm, unanswerable questions of his pupil as we both made our way down the smooth length of the waxed alley, pushing twelve hundred BB's with our hands while the owner watched.

"Tell me," Dad said in a very calm voice. "Why does one bring a million BB's to a bowling alley?"

"I didn't really bring them."

"I see. These are not yours?"

"Well, no, they're mine. They just fell out of my shirt pocket."

"And how did they get into your shirt pocket?"

"I put them there this morning. But I didn't intentionally bring them bowling."

"Offhand, I would say that what you intended to do doesn't really matter, does it? It happened because you didn't think ahead. Now these BB's are all over the place and you're going to pick up each one of them."

My family didn't get around to a lot of bowling after that. Mom's favorite sport was bridge. Her family's values emerged from a Victorian era when, at worst, women perspired. And they never appeared to compete. Bridge prompted no perspiration. It was legal ladylike competition among women. See, the women weren't really competing; it was the cards. That was a typically oblique feminine tactic. I preferred the up-front, in-your-face kind of competition. Why wait around for someone to guess the point when you could stick it right up their nose? But bridge also offered endless opportunities for Mom to chat with other ladies. At one of the bimonthly gatherings when one woman had to leave early, my mother pressed me into service as a fourth at her table. But I fell asleep during the instructions.

I don't recall much chatting with my mother, casually exchanging idle information or observations and learning about each other and life in the process. My father and I didn't chat idly either. But we talked a great deal, the way men must, about very specific things and always while doing something else so we weren't wasting time simply talking. There has to be a point to everything said. If you don't have a point to make, an insightful observation to share, or a thoughtful question to ask, keep your mouth shut. No need to hand out any examples of stupidity; there were enough floating around the world already.

In those days—actually, throughout our lives together—I could ask my Dad about anything I wanted, as long as the question showed some thought. Dumb questions drew dumb looks or, worse, silence. One series of little boy questions about the stars led to our taking a museum's father-son course on astronomy. This led to our construction of a telescope and then to a partial map of the stars that hung over rural northeastern Ohio in those days. The stars kept moving, however, which caused some duplication in my drawings, which prompted Dad to point out some books explaining operation of the heavens, which led me to decide to become an astronomer, which lasted two years. There was genuine excitement in trying to fathom the unfathomable with him. The answers didn't matter; the process of searching together did.

Mainly, I wanted to be just like Dad—mustachioed, strong, and tall; five-foot-eight was way up there from the point of view of four-foot-two. He was quiet, too, and seemed to know pretty much everything there was to know about anything that mattered. Dad didn't speak much around other people, until later when the company paid for him to study on Tuesday nights with someone named

Dale Carnegie. Then, all of a sudden, he was telling every-body in sight the kinds of stories or jokes that I had often heard. Or he'd make one of those short sarcastic comments that caused my little legs to crumble I was laughing so hard. Dad loved to see me laugh. He couldn't help smiling then himself and I could see the neat gap between his front teeth that enabled him to shoot that familiar stream of water when we went swimming. Dad came from the George Gobel school of comic delivery: Anything said plainly with a straight face was six times funnier because the listener discovers the humor himself.

But around me, Dad had always joked and talked as much as I wanted. Hey, Dad, tell me about growing up in a stone house; it was so cold on winter mornings that he had to break the ice in the washbowl. Tell me about playing rugby; no substitutions allowed, so you had to play even when hurt or else you'd let your teammates down. Tell me about mountain climbing in France; meals were bread and chocolate, which sounded great, and hard-boiled eggs, which didn't. And sometimes they slept in nets hanging under rock ledges, which sounded scary. Nothing is scary, he said, if you study and practice and know what you're doing. So he bought some ropes and for several Sundays we trooped through nearby woods tying all sorts of knots and clambering up and down some pretty tall cliffs and ledges.

Looking down some of those drops before descending, I thought they looked rather frightening. "Then don't look down," he suggested. There was no way out with him just because things got tough or looked tough. So down I went backwards. And when he got down, too, we had a chocolate bar to celebrate. All of which led to some pretty exciting tales in Monday's Show-and-Tell session.

There were some rules with Dad. *Never* lie was the big one. If I ever let a lie be sealed with an ensuing handshake, then the world or something very big would end. Also animals. They were very important to a man's life. Yes, they were fun to play with. But more importantly, having living things depend on you taught responsibility and understanding and compassion. My dogs and cats and horse, the birds all around, the rabbits, deer, and coons, probably even the weasels all had feelings and families and fears. One time when I forgot to feed the kittens, Dad didn't get angry. "You're getting to be a big boy," he said. "How do you think it would feel to be as tall as some monster's ankle and you only ate when he remembered to feed you?" I didn't get my meals until the animals had theirs. There were some priorities in life. That was the last time I forgot.

The first time a pet of mine died I was devastated. And I guess Dad was, too, because he cried as well. We had adopted that St. Bernard together. "Everything dies sometime, son. Dogs, cats, trees, people, plants."

"I don't care about plants."

"Sometimes it's just sooner than we'd like."

Pause.

"But it hurts so much."

"Yes, I know. I hurt, too. That means you really love him. And he loved you very much. You'll always have his memory."

"But I don't want a memory. I want him."

"Well, we don't always get what we want in life. And memories aren't so bad to have, Andy. Better than nothing. Life goes on, son."

"I don't care."

"It has to."

"I don't care."

"Well, you better start caring. You've got a lot to do in life."

"What? Like what?"

"I don't know. That's the mystery. It's exciting. Don't you want to know what you were meant to do?"

We decided that what I was meant to do right then was bang some nails into the barn. He'd taught me that, too— how to hammer so that at least half the blows hit the nail squarely on the head. And which way screws turn to go in—and out. The way to get ahead, he said, was to think ahead. Yes indeed, an eight-penny nail is nowhere near as strong as one the size of a railroad spike. But don't you think a spike might split wood that's only this thick? And hey, knucklehead, check the gas tank *before* you try to start the mower.

Poker and bargaining for a new car aside, I never saw Dad play any sports, except golf at the annual company picnic. I went once. The other men in plaid pants genuinely seemed to like Dad, too. He played golf once a year. I could tell he was pretty uncomfortable. I left.

But he and I competed regularly, everything from eating Life Savers quickly to just running or swimming. At first, I couldn't beat him. Then I didn't want to. But I did have to do my best to meet the expectations of Coach Dad.

Every night in good weather we played baseball. He was one team; I was the other. A hit this far was a single. One over there was a double, over there was a triple, and way back there was a homer. Three strikes. Three outs. We played a couple of innings each evening, carrying the score over, even running a best four-of-seven Yard Series. We shot some baskets together, although his bad eye made the score unusually close in that game. And we bet on every single Cleveland Browns game, twenty-five cents riding on each final score, year in and year out. I always had the Browns. He'd cheer for the other team, any other team. "Why don't you cheer for the same team?" my mother regularly suggested; she hated family friction. We'd look at her and then at each other and, shaking our heads, chalk it up to some genetic problem.

Backing the Browns in those days meant I would net as much as $1.50 to $2.00 per year, plus exhibition games. A better income certainly than my report card produced at times.

Sometimes Dad and I would go to an actual Browns game; it was too cold for Mom. The stadium holds eighty

thousand people; my mother would have said eighty-thou-
sand-odd people. I had never seen so many people in one
place, certainly not at a baseball game. Football games had
fewer cigars, or maybe it was just a stronger wind.

The first time I heard that many people erupt at once—
actually, I felt it—I stopped watching the game to watch
the crowd. It was such a visceral Technicolor experience.
A little frightening, but it attracted me. I looked at Dad.
He smiled. He raised his eyebrows—"How about that?"
Wow! The unity of so many different people. The intoxi-
cating unanimity. I cheered, too. How could you not?
Milt Plum had just handed the ball to Jim Brown around
right end. Gene Hickerson was out in front. And very good
things were about to happen.

With Jim (being as good a Browns fan as I am, I can call
him by his first name, although we have never been closer
than half the width of Cleveland Stadium), good things
usually did happen. He'd rumble this way or that, stop
suddenly, cut back. Pursuing bodies would fly by, tackling
empty air or a leg that disappeared. Finally, three or four
bad guys would gang up to fall Our Hero. He would lay
there on the ground motionless for an extra moment. The
home crowd held its breath. Slowly, too slowly for our
team's collective health, he rose and trotted back to the
huddle. Phew! He did it every time. And every time we
watched. And every time he got up. The public suspense
and shared relief brought us all together. He was great.
That shows on the films. But those mutual moments of
suspense and happiness were even greater.

I have long sensed that the real importance of clubs was
not the belonging but the knowing for sure there are others
who do not belong. I mean, if everybody's in the club,
what's the point of the club, right? Well, there was no one
there that Sunday who was not cheering. I wanted to belong, too, to share that allegiance. I might have a math
quiz on Monday and I'd never know if Eleanor really liked
me. These others might fight with their wives and get laid

off on Tuesday because the business of making steel and so many other things was changing in disturbing ways. And very few of us had ever played the game of football, or it had been so long since we played that we only remembered the good parts—and those better than they were. But who cares? They were our memories to mold and amend as desired. And, by golly, today we would savor our mutual membership in the stands. We were winners! Living life as viewed from the good seats.

Over the years the vividness of this experience faded. I did not live in Cleveland. And the thrill of paying a large sum to sit in the cold with thousands of former inmates while watching someone like Atlanta play New Orleans was just not there. It was so much easier simply to sit at home with my own white popcorn, an unlimited supply of Coca-Cola, and instant replays (not to mention warm feet and an odor-free bathroom) and watch my team perform between the commercials.

Our country has long had civic allegiances, the kind of superficial pride that requires some television audience members to burst into applause at the mention of their hometown, or any town. (How can there always be someone from every town mentioned at every show?) And, of course, I was generally aware of the intensifying team allegiances—and the public's need to flaunt them, most often through wardrobe statements. A fair number of urban murder victims got that way because of their unwillingness to give up a team jacket coveted by another fan.

Other Americans by the millions now live on streets or hallways where they only know their neighbor by sight. That kind of transient impersonality doesn't seem to matter much, because in four or five years they'll move again anyway. With an increasingly homogenized national culture, no matter where they are physically, these folks can belong, forever, to their favorite team through team newspapers, fan clubs, and, naturally, wearing the squad's commercial logo. The fortunes of a city of hundreds of thousands of people can even seem to rise and fall according to the athletic success of their team of five dozen athletic mercenaries and coaches. Some millionaire used car dealer may hold the formal title to the franchise and the check for all the TV money is made out in that owner's name, leading that person of substantial richness to think not unreasonably that he or she owns the team. But to millions of people who have invested cheers, groans, devotions, not to mention ticket and sweatshirt money and their unadulterated allegiance over many years, that team belongs to them.

As a result, today, civic and team identities have become merged in most professional football communities. It's hard to miss that intensifying identification when, for instance, the concert time of the Chicago Symphony is changed from mid-afternoon to lunchtime on their Super Bowl Sunday and then the musicians all come on stage wearing tuxedos and Chicago Bear stocking caps. They even sell fishing lures in the colors of each NFL team. All of this, of course, seems ridiculous and crass in a commercialized American way—until it involves your team.

And then one January many, many long years after that Jim Brown run, one of my many bosses telephoned. He wanted me to help cover the next weekend's football playoff game in Cleveland. Gee, I said with chilling visions of the wind-whipped upper deck overlooking Lake Erie without Dad, I'd really rather watch the game. "Oh, you can watch the game from the press box," he said. "I only want you to interview the Browns players in their locker room after the game."

That, I said, I was pretty sure I could fit into my otherwise impossible schedule. I took my family along for the fun. The first inkling of something unusual came the day before the game on the downtown streets of Cleveland where every living soul was wearing something orange and brown. Smiling strangers greeted smiling strangers with an open friendliness straight out of some phony, precisely choreographed Broadway musical about small-town America. Buildings were decorated. Horns were honked. Whoops were ubiquitous. Hands were shaken. High-fives exchanged, even hugs. The street-level joy was contagious. And all this over one little football game.

Sure, it was going to be on television, which magnifies everything with its lights and Cylopean vision. But lots of games have been aired since the first live radio broadcast of a game on November 22, 1930, from New Haven, Connecticut, a no-doubt stirring struggle between two traditional powerhouses, which Harvard won, 12–0, over Yale. The difference now was that we were about to experience a playoff game on the other side of the camera, which relatively few fans do. To be sure, the average crowd at any professional football game is three times the average attendance at a professional baseball game. And every year more than 17.5 million people buy tickets to see nearly 250 National Football League games. But so great is the addictive involvement of television that more people than that watch a single Monday Night game on TV.

Live, on camera, turns out to be very much different than live, on site, in person. Electricity was in the air as I walked up the familiar old cement ramps where I had once trod, very excited, in my black PF Flyers, hurrying to keep up with Dad. People hustled about urgently as if their plane was about to leave. Even the souvenir vendors had little television sets on their tables so they could watch their goods right there and the game just a hundred yards away.

Turn right, then up a narrower ramp that opened onto the seats, and WOW! The noise! The lights! The people! The colors! The grass was terribly green for January; up close, it was clearly spray-painted, but it looked great for the cameras. And the paying spectators had become part of the show, unknowingly at first and then willingly providing the dramatic background noise and the scenes of crazed happiness on cue. The simple signal igniting the virus of exhibitionism was to have the nearest camera swing across one section of seats. This prompted some to wave a six-foot cardboard sign they just happened to have brought with them while everyone else held up the obligatory fore-finger. (Someday, just for fun, I want to see someone supporting the losers hold up two fingers—"We're No. 2, We're No. 2." And then, although we can't hear him for lack of a microphone, that same guy will make television history by being the first to say, "Hi, Dad.")

Many of these unpaid football cast members had told friends where they would be sitting should they have the good fortune to have their existence endorsed by a TV camera and the folks at home would get excited because they thought they saw their yellow jacket. Just being at a game, any game, that was televised could easily elevate its importance—and the importance of the spectator when, come Monday morning, he reminded co-workers of his attendance the previous day at the game that was the most important of the season, until next weekend.

For the first fifty-six minutes of this playoff game, I was the picture of decorum in the press box, where cheering is prohibited as unprofessional. So I ate a couple more hot dogs than usual; who would know but me? So my notes were incomplete because I was silently rooting; I wasn't covering the actual game anyway. I was rather subdued, in fact, when with barely four minutes remaining in the game, the usher lead the contingent of locker-room reporters down to the sidelines to be in position to wash into the locker room with the defeated Cleveland players. We—that is, they—were down by ten points to some team from New York.

By the time I got to the bog that surrounded the end zone, the Browns were driving. Wouldn't it be nice if they scored at least once more? I was right there on the field, almost exactly where Bobby Avila dove and scooped and threw to Vic Wertz. Too bad I was doing just a newspaper article on football and not a book. I looked up. Suddenly, there was a Cleveland fullback running into my face. Damn, these guys were bigger in real life! He had mud hanging off his face mask. His fingers were bloody. Some red stained his once-white kneepads. Another working man just doing his job. He ran right by me, puffing. In the cold, I could see and feel his breath. He winked. The cast member winked at me.

Wait. Wait! Holy cow, he had just scored a touchdown. The Browns had just scored a touchdown! My God, the stadium was going crazy. Many thousands of people yelling and stomping. The Browns were down by four now. Could they do it? In under three minutes? Silently, I hoped. I looked at the cop next to me. He wasn't doing his job either. "I don't know," he said, his voice full of optimism. "I don't know."

The extra point was good. I called it first. It sailed right over my head. The officials agreed. Down by three now. I looked at the cop, now my soul brother. "Okay, okay," I said. "We'll take it."

"You bet," he said.

New York's ball. The clock was running—the clock was running. But our defense held. They did it. New York had to punt. Had to. Unless. No, they punted. Okay. Under two minutes. How far to go, what, eighty yards? Hard to tell from the playing field. The game looks all scattered and chaotic from there, not the precise patterns and logical flow seen from the vantage of a living room couch. Eighty yards was probably too far. Maybe not. We only needed three points to force an overtime.

"A field goal would do it," I told the cop. Now, he could have replied, "Yes, thank you so very much. I know how to count to three. And I have known that since my days at a city elementary school that no longer exists." But as strangers we were now bonded by our athletic allegiance to this sport and hope for our team, for ourselves.

"Yup," he said. "Just three, baby. Just three."

The stadium was going wild. Yelling and stomping. C'mon, let's go here. Why weren't they playing the game? Why was the clock stopped?

"Commercials," said the cop, a stadium veteran. We all stood around for two more minutes until the watching world's unseen millions rejoined us. Life could begin again. And the crowd roared on cue.

Finally, the whistle. Play began. Things did not go well. Third down. Gotta do it now. Nope. Fourth down. Well, what the hell. Go for it. One more chance. And, it's no good. Damn! But wait. A penalty flag. Yes, oh yes, thank you Higher Being. First down. Another one. Oh, yes, do it, guys, do it! A little farther. A little more. Only seconds left. Stop the clock. Bring in the kicker. This was the reject from another team. Now was his chance for redemption. Fly high with the suspended breaths of eighty thousand crazed fans. Or die 'neath the groans of the same mob.

The ball is snapped. It's down. It's up. It's—it's—no good. Is it? No, wait, it's good. It's good! He made it! WE DID IT! Pandemonium in the stadium. Jubilation on the sidelines, well, one of them anyway. I'm high-fiving the policeman and everyone else in sight. You'd have thought we won the universe's championship instead of the right to play fifteen more minutes of sudden death overtime. First to score wins.

Oh, God, here we go again. I wasn't sure the deity dabbled in sudden-death overtimes on cold afternoons in northeast Ohio. I know He usually deals just with the Big Picture. But from the western end zone of Cleveland Stadium, the immediate issue seemed like a pretty big picture right now. Just in case, I lofted a prayer or three up there. What could it hurt? If He was out, it was undeliverable.

I don't remember ever feeling so excited. When children are born, that is exciting, to be sure. But that excitement is tempered by terror. And those moments are invested with import; it's life and the other thing. This game was pure excitement. It really involved nothing of substance. So it was safe to invest my entire self. If they won, we would revel in the reflected glory. If they lost, big disappointment, but so what really? But "so what" was not the expression leaping to my lips at that moment. We were on the brink now of winning part of a regional championship of one-half of a national football league that wasn't even recognized as a serious sport in the rest of the world. I was riding the crest of destiny here—well, all right, along with the players, too. We were all in this together. This was great.

I looked up to where Dad and I used to sit. He was gone by then. But there was my own family sitting several rows down. I waved my arm. Nothing. I waved both arms. Flag signals over my head. Jumping up and down. Look at me, family. Look at me, a middle-aged kid momentarily freed of inhibitions by a sport and his team. I'm down on the playing field of one of the longest games in NFL history. See me? One child did. He pointed. The others saw, too. They waved to me. I waved back. We waved some more.

I cheer, therefore, I am.

There was nothing sudden about that overtime. It ended tied, too. The Browns missed one kick, probably The Chance to put it away. But New York did, too. These guys were exhausted down here. So was I, from just cheering. Finally, deep into the second OT, my Brownies did it. The same kicker re-redeemed himself. That ball sailed right over my head one more time.

Oh, yes. Oh, yes. I'm hugging a strange cop. Sodden, muddy players are all around me, yelling uncontrollably. Some cry, rubbing their eyes with fingers coated in filthy tape. The locker room stinks of steamy sweat. My frozen glasses are thoroughly fogged in the showered humidity. My body, still coated in winter gear, is giving itself a shower. There is nowhere to move. I'm crouched down between two other reporters' knees, straining to hear the historic words of one player in this epic battle that I now don't remember the year of.

Within an hour, I had regained my sanity, if not my voice. I had written my story on the kicker and his joy. And within a few hours I was a hundred miles away descending back into my pastel life of comfort, distanced reality, and instant replays. But what had happened back there on the sideline? What had unleashed those primal forces of pride? There surely was more to this than a fullback's fleeting wink or a troubled community's desperate need to be a winner. Where had all that vivid hope and fury come from? The most-watched television shows in history are football games. What is this peculiar hold of sport, this sport, on a national psyche? It's colorful. It can be suddenly dramatic, almost always clear-cut. But how could football be so much more than a game to so many people? To my family? to me, who had not played the game in, what, twenty-five years?

☐ ☐ ☐

I remember football in my childhood corner of Ohio countryside as more than a sport. It was an integral part of life's rhythms, which became more noticeable after we moved from the ever-gray cement city to the green and brown country that changed by the season, even by the day or the hour at times, as the wildflowers awakened to the sunshine. The year began with a very long, very snowy winter. Then came a precious spring so brimming with promise that even a little Indians fan could find hope in the new nests overflowing with feathered life. Summer came like a huge wet towel thrown over the county to hold in all the heat and moisture for the corn, which you could almost hear growing up through the black dirt. Summer was followed by the season of football, which contained Labor Day, Back-to-School day, Homecoming, Halloween, the grade school Pilgrim pageant, and Thanksgiving, if your school made the playoffs, which mine never did.

Many people breathed football. Students went to see friends play and be seen by nonplaying friends. Adults went to the Friday night games even after their sons and daughters had graduated from the team and the cheerleading squad. It reminded them of those old days, or perhaps even the older days when it was they who were out on the field in delightful agony over third down and one. Grade school youngsters went to the high school games and played their own untimed, uncoordinated games of padless tackle football in the grass just beyond the real end zone. Even some of the grade school girls played.

There were other sports, of course. There was something called basketball, which was obviously invented by Indiana because so many of its towns didn't contain eleven boys. Soccer had yet to become fashionable among young parents who planned their taxes, babies, foreign car purchases, and babies' educations with the programmable precision possible with home computers. The springtime signup meeting for Little League always drew a good crowd, although the teams dwindled drastically as the family vacation season began.

The high school coaches were also, not coincidentally, the phys ed teachers, which gave them a chance to scout countless dodgeball games for the most aggressive, the most nimble, the quickest, the biggest. By seventh grade, these men were combing through the physically coordinated youngsters, feeding their fragile egos with dreams of someday playing on the varsity.

At the top of one Christmas wish list then was a football outfit with the long socks, the pant legs that ended fashionably just below the knee, the genuine cardboard thigh boards, the oversized shoulder pads, and the plastic helmet that wobbled around on my head like a dying top. I loved it. Football shoes were too expensive when there was no chance of playing for several years. So I wore my hightop paratrooper boots. And on that frigid Christmas day I ran around our back field in my new football outfit, making endless circles and zigzags, calling meaningless signals, giving fantasy handoffs and receiving them, tumbling on the frozen field and bouncing back up, lobbing touchdown passes and catching them, too, in front of an invisible crowd of exultant thousands who got so delirious over my moves that I had to stop for lunch.

Dad marked some yard lines on that grassy stubble so I could measure my punts, which sometimes went where I had hoped, though I didn't know why. Friends came over and we tossed each other wobbling but game-saving throws that grew even more dramatic in the telling over the potatoes at dinner.

From the vantage point of the south window in the children's reading room of the village library, I saw the future. And I wanted very badly to attend the upcoming battles. Through that old window pane on weekday afternoons I could watch the varsity players pound down the pavement of Division Street on their way to practice. Full of energy and muscle and the optimism of a new week that sprang like a spring flower each autumn Monday, they sometimes chanted rhythmically as their metal cleats hit the sidewalk. This may have had more to do with being seen than with generating team spirit, but it worked. From the height of four feet and the vantage point of twelve years of age, I was impressed mightily, even if I was still there to see them straggle, exhausted, back to the locker room nearly three hours later. Their helmets were still blue. But these boys were not chanting then.

I wanted to do that very much. I did not yet see the players as teenage knights venturing out once a week to joust in legalized aggression with the equally youthful representatives of another nearby educational fortress, all of them cloaking their fears and uncertainties beneath cumbersome pads and colored jerseys. Of course, I didn't have even an inkling of what it would entail or mean to me and, later, my own boys to play or, rather, live football. I had no idea how to play it, what I might be good at, what I might have to learn to do and overcome, to endure and enjoy, to forget and savor, and how much faster the game is to play than to watch. I was so naive (or maybe determined) that I don't even remember being aware of the possibility of failure. And I certainly had no clue how deeply a game—and the men who taught it—would permeate the habits and thought processes of my later life. I had always liked to play; children innately do. Football was the next step in becoming a man. I just wanted to be a part of it then. There seemed to me to be a growing amount of chores involved in growing up. Now, finally, in football there came a part of growing up that was fun. Football made life so vivid, so much richer than what had been normal. If life is a game, then football was basic training. And I was eager to enlist.

□ □ □

For better or worse, I have never been family-famous for half-measures. My wife says this is a prize-winning understatement. If a little dedication was good, a little more was better. And a lot more was a lot better. My father always told me I could do anything I had to do, and I certainly had to play football. I believed Dad. And that made that pronouncement come true.

The coaches, those often overweight fountains of clichés, would waddle up and down the rows of young men performing painful exercises, saying, "You gotta want it." Well, I wanted it, all right. So intense was this unharnessed desire of mine that had these gatekeepers of maledom known then how badly I wanted to play football, they might have benched me for fear of what I might wreak. Or made me captain immediately.

There were no little kids football leagues in the hometown of my youth. So any football before ninth grade was strictly pickup, the most dangerous kind. One sunny Saturday morning along about seventh or eighth grade some of the fathers bowed to the pressures of their boys (and perhaps their fears of what might happen without some parental supervision) and organized a game, sort of. All week long it was *the* topic of conversation at school, as we announced and argued what position we each would play. Everybody, it seemed, wanted to play star quarterback or star halfback, with emphasis on the star part. I did not. I had no idea how to play either position, or any position except maybe guard. I knew how guards sometimes faked a defensive lineman, but I wasn't sure really where each player stood.

So I thought defense sounded best; I still do. You know, less rules. Reacting to someone else's moves. Creating chaos in their puny plan of attack. Not many points to be put on the scoreboard that way for the good guys, unless you did something very bold or imaginative, which would be neat. But what could that be? I had no idea how to play defense. But it also seemed safer, didn't put you out front to make a glaring mistake. Shows how little I knew. I liked the sound of linebacker. It sounded strong. I wanted to be strong, or at least feel strong.

We all stood around on the shiny, wet grass that morning, incredibly awkward and ill at ease, but eager, very eager. Like horses before the starting gate. When they opened that starting gate, we might run the wrong way. But we'd do it with such eagerness.

The uniforms that day had little uniformity. They were pulled together from attics and brothers. Everybody had a helmet, of course. They were all colors of the rainbow. And shoulder pads of varying sizes bulged beneath shirts that were not made to cover such artificial bulk. So the shirt bottoms rode up above the belly button, which is quite the thing now in football fashion but we didn't know that back then. So, as our mommies suggested, we wore other shirts underneath to keep our tummies warm.

Team colors (also hats) have always been very important before doing battle. Okay, so they couldn't afford real uniforms for the Revolution. But by the time the Blue and the Gray fought, there was the red, white, and blue and they were handing out Congressional Medals of Honor just for capturing the other side's colors.

Of course, there was no color coordination by teams on my first football-playing Saturday because there were no teams. So every shirt was a different color, often having something to do with a father's college. A few of us had pants that looked like football pants and maybe we even had one or two of the proper pads within. The others wore blue jeans, which would never be that clean again.

Everybody just wore high-topped canvas shoes, which were called tennis shoes then because none of us played tennis. But that's what all canvas shoes were called before our society learned from a thoughtful tennis shoe manufacturer that we needed a different pair of canvas shoes for every conceivable athletic activity. Plus, of course, some other style canvas shoe, laughably called cross-trainers, with colored stripes that may be used for multiple purposes, even walking. The early 1950s were black-and-white times, so we just wore one kind of rubber-soled shoe. They were black because black enabled you to run faster. I recall the girls had white sneakers for gym class and some were red, which was a fruity color on your feet but okay if it was on your jacket.

But there were no girls around on that Saturday because football was a serious business for guys and guys don't like girls around at times of serious business, especially if the guys don't have a clue what the hell they're doing in that serious business—which we didn't. In fact, the athletic field was behind a thick row of trees out on the edge of town. Very convenient.

I recall a couple of fathers trying to do some football teaching, which was very kind. Also, it was hopeless for two reasons. Well, three actually. One, these dads were accustomed to talking to employees, who have a definite economic stake in listening and learning; we had no such stake. Instruction was just boring preliminaries before the good stuff of plain old running around. Second, this was Saturday, so we were set to play; nothing serious happened on Saturdays, except visits to the dentist's office and, one year, Confirmation classes. The latter coincided with the arrival of pimples, but none of this involved running around or fun. And third, these fathers were nice guys and all. They surely had supreme power in their houses and everything. Or the entire society lived with that fiction because appearance was important then. But these dads weren't coaches; you could tell by their long-sleeved shirts and pants with creases. Real coaches had an aura of physical toughness about them, stronger because it was implied more than used. Everyone had seen a coach abruptly pin some troublemaker against the gym wall to have a brief, quiet, one-way chat because the kid wasn't showing respect for his elders. Maybe some skinny science teacher would take that kid's lipping-off, or the math instructor with enough wavy hair to be a violin player. But coaches didn't have to; their degrees were in phys ed, which I used to think meant they dished out education physically. The coaches could see those undisciplined little troublemaking peckers a mile away. Ten to one, the boy's parents were divorced or the father traveled too much, so the rest of the world was going to pay for it. Girl's coaches were usually short women with even shorter hair; they looked like, if you gave them trouble, you'd get a quick chop to the throat or somewhere worse. Boy's coaches looked like they could take just one of their beefy forearms, catch you under the chin, and probably send you right through the wall. They didn't, of course. This was not because some underemployed lawyer who didn't go to Ohio State had warned them against it, but because then you'd miss Friday's game. Coaches just looked like they could deck you. The dads of other kids didn't.

Coaches also didn't wear ties with wool sports coats and leather elbows. In fact, coaches looked uncomfortable in their ties; at work they wore white tennis shirts with metal whistles on black cords (not white). These tennis shirts had useless little breast pockets with no room for anything larger than your old aunt's hankie. They also had short sleeves,

even in the winter when the cold drafts blowing down a
junior high hallway seemed sufficiently strong to move a
disobedient locker door. Short sleeves showed off coaches'
muscles more. Dads were more interested in mental muscle
because that's what they thought they had. So Dads in
short-sleeved tennis shirts standing on an athletic field blowing whistles hanging on a white shoelace lifted from one of
their daughter's ice skates were not intimidating sights igniting instant obedience.

After the useless instruction came the time to choose up
teams. Even though this was football, choosing teams was
always accomplished through the time-honored baseball bat
method, which, like the arcane rankings of childhood's
dares, double dares, and triple dares, seems inordinately
complex at this moment but back then was the surest, most
indisputably equitable method to avoid playground dis-
putes. Knowing that teams were to be chosen, one father
had naturally brought a baseball bat to football practice.
The ritual involved the head dad appointing two team captains. One captain tossed the baseball bat to the other captain, who caught it with one hand. From where the catching
captain's hand gripped the wood, the first captain applied
his hand. And the two boys alternated grips up the shaft
to the nub of the handle. The last captain to get at least
two fingers below the nub got first choice. Now that you
understand this evolutionary process, you can see why the
fourth finger and the pinky have developed over time into
the two thinnest fingers.

Now, choosing sides had a certain predictability to it.
Regardless of who was captain, the first few choices were
always the same young athletes whose coordination skills
had arrived first and elevated them to the peak level of
team desirability and, not coincidentally, teen leadership.
Everyone who was even semi-conscious knew how well they
performed from seeing them in gym class and, before the
age of specialization, the assumption was that all athletic
skills carried over to all sports; life too, the coaches said.

These skills had yet to be translated into substantial salaries or athletic scholarships, which sometimes were the same thing, it turns out. But they did confer considerable teen status. And the swift knew their superior ranking; they often swaggered. This process, I am sure, is how the NFL draft evolved.

Anyway, the seventh-grade choosing went very quickly in the first few rounds. Everyone as yet unchosen silently offered their entire beings to the temporarily all-powerful captains. Some choosees displayed their nervousness by fidgeting or pleading with their eyes to the captains. You always assumed you'd be picked in this round. Well, maybe not this one, but certainly the next. Or the next. Well, this time for sure. Or this time. There, see, I told ya.

Of course, as there are always first and second choices, there are always last choices, too, and second to last, which have suddenly become desperate to avoid the ignominy of actually being last choice. Through a fairly accurate measurement of physical and socialization skills, last and second-to-last were painful places to be. However, as time passed, those former kids wreaked their revenge; they helped invent computers and computer software to impose on their former big-shot playground captains an entirely new and baffling language of command keys, "merges," and "interfaces," which their tormentors from teendom would have to learn in order to survive.

Now that the football preparations had consumed so long that it was nearly time to go home for lunch, we could start the game.

It was chaos. Absolute chaos. These kids had studied their parents perfectly at the Autumn Organizational Meeting of the PTA. Our football game that day defined confusion. I had thought that being elected captain automatically instilled in someone the skills necessary for leadership. This was, of course, a fatal fallacy that had been revealed during the Civil War nearly a century before. But it being fall, my history class was still laboring through the

Puritans with their funny white collars, so how could I know that? Eleven people in the huddle had at least eleven ideas of what play should be run, and each idea seemed to focus on giving its inventor the ball. In normal football, tackles and guards rarely got the ball intentionally. But that day they each wanted it. The center thought it would be tricky not to give the quarterback the ball but just keep it himself and run straight ahead. Certainly tricky, though illegal, he was told.

"Why is it illegal?" he asked.

"It just is," said the quarterback, who wasn't really sure but wanted the ball himself.

"But why? They won't be expecting it."

"C'mon," said four other guys simultaneously. They wanted the ball, too, but at least that shut up the center.

"Now, here's what we'll do," said the quarterback. And he outlined a play that involved three handoffs and got the ball back in his hands in time for the applause. This proposal, designed as its designer spoke, neglected to mention what the other seven players might be doing, which gave several of them an opportunity to launch amendments, which required explanations and amendments and amendments of the amendments by which time half the players had forgotten what they were supposed to do in the first place. It had looked so simple on television. A bunch of guys get together in a huddle, decide what to do, and then do it.

Ten minutes into the huddle we had yet to decide on the first play, let alone run it. The defensive players, who had been waiting patiently, eagerly, with no need to prepare for anything except to converge violently on the guy with the ball, were now sitting down, chewing a blade of grass or making whistles with them between their thumbs. Some sought to stomp ants. The fathers were discussing lawn mowers.

Finally, the offense was ready. The players wandered to the line of scrimmage, not exactly reeking of confidence.

Half had their hands in their pockets. One by one, they kind of bent over like they had seen the pros do. The quarterback said, "Ready. Set. Go!" And nothing happened. The right guard and tackle went to stand up again. The left side thought the play had started; they charged ahead. The center thought he was late. He hiked the ball. The quarterback wasn't sure this was legal. He dropped the ball. The running backs, not looking, went into their movements with a precision exceeded only by its irrelevance. The quarterback crawled over to the ball, started to get up with it, and was buried by ten guys. The fathers, who belatedly realized the game had begun, blew their whistles impressively.

We had lost four yards.

This disaster did not appear in the Guinness Book of Firsts, but in the course of one single play eleven boys had managed to commit twelve mistakes. Time to assess blame.

"Way to go, Lindeman."

"Nice move, Malcolm."

"Yeah, well I didn't see you hitting anybody."

"How could I get over there with your big feet in the way?"

"Yeah? Well, my big feet are gonna crunch your face right now."

"Boys. Boys. Boys," said the fathers. "C'mon now. We came here to play football. Now let's have some fun."

"How can we have any fun when Hunt there doesn't even know what to do?"

"Boys! Boys! Get back there. Now call another play."

The defense was still celebrating as if school had just ended, which made it worse. We could turn our heads away and pretend we felt no mortification. But the cheers and mocking comments, exaggerated for our benefit, still seeped in through the earholes of our helmets.

One play into the first football game of our lives, some of us were ready to give up.

Time to simplify. "Okay," said the quarterback, who was eager to celebrate something. "we'll pass. You run out there and I'll throw it to you. Everybody else block." Okay, now we were on track. This was going to work. They'd never think of a pass.

The start of the play was a little ragged again; the quarterback had forgotten to announce a signal. But no one had thought to bring along any penalty flags that day either. So the play continued and the wobbly pass fell harmlessly to earth yards from any player on either team.

"C'mon, Wilkens!" the quarterback whined. "I told you to run over there."

"No, you didn't. You said over here."

"No, I didn't."

"Yes, you did."

"Prove it!"

"Wanna make something of it?"

"Boys. Boys. C'mon. Things don't always go well at first. Have another huddle."

Third down. One more chance to make fourteen yards. One of the fathers had decided to stand where we would have to reach. Otherwise, we'd have to punt the ball away. Yards look a lot longer when you're playing than when you're watching.

"Let's kick on third down," said Pfeiffer.

"Yeah," another agreed. "That'll fool 'em."

It was, to be sure, an unorthodox move. But kicking unnecessarily soon had one great advantage: It would let the other pathetic team lose for a while. But how does a team execute a surprise third-down kick when they have never practiced any kind of kick? And, anyway, who was our kicker? Someone said their dad had taught them to kick. That boy was promptly named official kicker. The center was reminded that he should hike the ball all the way back past the quarterback's legs to the secret kicker. To make sure the surprise kick secret did not get out on the way back to the line of scrimmage, every member of the offense reminded every other member not to say anything by going, "Shhhhh. Shhhhh. Shhhhh."

The center remembered what to do, although the ball had to go the last couple of yards on the ground. The kicker got the kick off. It was no boomer. But it went a lot farther than we had gotten it on the ground.

The other team was, indeed, surprised. And delighted. They interpreted the third-down kick as a mistake. "Thanks a lot," they said.

"We meant to kick," we shot back.

"Thanks a lot."

It took them only five minutes to plan their first play. They lost a yard, which ignited adolescent recriminations on that team and overjoyous celebrations on my squad. Like Dad had said, what goes around comes around. Now I understood. We really rubbed it in with the celebrating. Gee, it was great!

Their second play went outside the end. Outside ours, too, unfortunately. This being only the twelfth year and the fifth football play of our lives, none of us knew anything about anticipation. Oh, we anticipated Christmas all right. But that required no thinking, just watching the calendar and waiting. Anticipation in life, I began to learn that morning, required close readings of patterns or evidence and then careful projections into the future. Our defensive end, who probably wasn't sure what his position was called let alone what it entailed, was just watching the ball like they do on TV. By the time he realized the ballcarrier would pass beyond his reach, other enemies were in the way. He was blocked. And the way was open for a long gain. It wasn't planned as well as it looked, I was sure. But the scoreboard doesn't say: Good Guys 0, Enemy 14, although 7 of them came on a fluke play.

The run was a long one, though not a touchdown. About five guys caught up with the runner by the sidelines and dragged him down. I arrived late but wanted to make sure and to be involved. So I jumped on the pile and sat atop the writing bulk of adolescents. A whistle blew.

"Piling on!" yelled one father.

"What's piling on?"

"Fifteen yards!"

"It's a penalty?"

"Yes, my boy."

"For them or us?"

The father looked at me, patiently. "Against *you*," he said.

"What?" I screamed. This was a father, not mine, but still an authority figure. So I couldn't argue with him directly.

"Did you ever hear of piling on?" I asked one teammate. He never had. "Did you?" I asked another. He shook his head. "Did you ever hear of piling on?" I asked a third. No, he said. Well, there you have it; four know-nothing kids against one know-everything dad, who marched off roughly fifteen yards anyway. No one there had ever heard of piling on as a penalty because probably no one in history had ever been dumb enough to do it.

Darn. It turns out this game of football had rules, just like school and arithmetic and church and lots of other stuff in life. So, okay, I'd learn the rules of football. But only football. I didn't care about all that other stuff.

We played another hour or so. It was a miracle no one was crippled. We had incomplete, inadequate equipment. No one was in football-shape. Everyone was doing what they thought they had seen some real football player do sometime somewhere. The word "technique" did not exist in our minds. The fathers probably went home, embarrassed, and when their wives asked how it went, they said simply, "Pretty good," which in husband-wife talk of the 1950s meant, "I don't ever want to talk about it again." These well-meaning men, who perhaps had dreamed of being small-time coaches as much as we had dreamed of being big-time players, tried to let the world, or their world anyway, forget the whole thing. The strategy worked; we never had another game like that.

But it really didn't matter. We were no longer football virgins. We were genuine players. Not very good players and way, way down on the food chain of football talent. But we had played.

☐ ☐ ☐

On Monday morning, I was so excited about getting to school that I couldn't wait for the bus. I jammed my books into the red-vinyl, Western Auto saddlebags and jumped on my ancient multicolored balloon-tire bike, the one I washed and decorated so carefully for Memorial Day parades. And I dashed down the four miles of country roads and elm-lined town streets to the imposing brick school that now has more annexes than main building. People think of schools for teenagers as a collection of classrooms where lessons are handed out by hardworking teachers with sturdy mimeograph machines. Partly true. But so much more teaching and learning goes on informally in the hallways, gyms, locker rooms, libraries, washrooms, and cafeterias. There, we each inadvertently offered up countless tentative observations to each other. They were received with respect or ridicule, silence or laughter, prompting others to present their uncertain observations and desires. From these repetitions we learned what was currently funny, stupid, cool, out-of-it, even what was teen-wise.

Sports—specifically football—were definitely cool. That is something that school boards, concerned over dropout rates, absenteeism, and other signs of our social malaise, ought to remember as they perform the now-annual ritual of budget sacrificing. There were bruised boys from our football game barging into school early that Monday morning who would normally seize upon any excuse, any alleged internal malfunction, to be tardy or absent.

We gathered in ostentatious huddles to relive the joys and amazing athleticism of the previous Saturday. Everyone had their own favorite memory or memories. We went on and on. Each memory by one sparked three more by others, who clamored for the floor in a very competitive verbal shoving match that would be repeated many years later over Monday lunch as these same males, now perhaps fathers themselves, competed to recount the best play they had seen on the previous day's game. Oh, you think that was good? Lemme tell you about the one, I think it was in the second quarter, when. . . .

It had taken only forty-eight hours for our Saturday morning game, which hadn't even been divided into quarters, to ascend the scale of neat (a word that was, over the years, to turn into awesome). Our game had become an epic encounter worthy of being enshrined in a book someday. You shoulda been there. The runs were darting, swift, and sure, the passes arrow-straight, the tackling stunning, the play-calling unerringly ingenious. The ref had made one really, really stupid penalty call that helped the other guys score some points. But other than that, the game was a definite classic worthy of the sepia tone it earned in our memory.

The guys who had played were puffed up by their importance, pleased by their survival, and warmed by their inclusion with like-minded fellows. It was a bond based on a shared interest that they just knew was prestigious. It felt very good, kind of dizzying. Just by listening, those who had not attended the big game felt smaller, left out, irrelevant for now. Unless they offered a hasty, credible excuse like having had a doctor's appointment or their mother not letting them play football, which earned some tight-lipped, head-nodding sympathy. Most of them vowed to play in the next game. They may still be waiting.

The girls couldn't help but overhear the excited discussions, which was no accident. They might normally have mocked the scene or sought to interrupt the discussions by walking by. But so eager were boys' pronouncements to each other that the future women picked up on the scene's strange import and let it pass in closely observed silence.

Before gym class we cornered the varsity football coach. The coach was very tall but built like a wrestler with one of those necks that looks more like a very short thigh. He liked seventh- and eighth-grade boys; they were the future of his teams. We surrounded him in the hall outside the Science room, where they always kept the doors closed to help confine the explosions of inept Einsteins. Grown men like being the Pied Piper. By ninth or tenth grade, it wasn't cool to lavish such eager attentions on adults. But we were only seventh- or eighth-grade cool. So we clamored like crazy.

"Hey, Coach. We had a football game on Saturday."

"Yeah, a regular game with penalties and punts and everything."

"Yeah, and Wilkens fumbled, too."

"Shut up!"

Coach kept walking for a while with our mob circling and stumbling in orbit around his bustling bulk. Finally, he stopped. He looked down. He smiled. "You had a football game, did you?"

"Yup."

Now that we had his attention, we had nothing to say. Absolutely nothing. We had said it all: We had a football game. That's all. It had seemed important that he know this. Period. Anyway, what could we possibly say to this major leader, the man who ran the entire high school football team on Friday night beneath all the bright lights? What could we, mere junior high school football wannabes, tell him in person that he hadn't already heard over his earphones on the sidelines? Why would he care about our game? Oh, God, what if he started really asking about it? Suddenly, we were all aghast at our impudence. We were keeping him from important things. We fell silent, scrambling as only a desperate teen mind can scramble for something meaningful to say. Anything.

"At the field up past the hockey pond."

"What?"

"That's where the game was."

He nodded knowingly.

Silence.

"What kind of offense did you guys run?"

What kind of offense?

"Uh, football? Yeah, it was a football offense."

"Well, I assumed that. I mean, was it a T or a wing?"

Silence.

Gee, look at the time. Almost time to change classes.

"A T." It was Dudley speaking. He never spoke. But here he was saying just two letters and saving our ass. I always said Dudley was a good guy.

"So you probably stuck to dives and crossbucks, I suppose."

More silence.

"Yeah. Dives and crossed bucks."

"Who was the QB?"

The what?

"Andrews was the quarterback."

"Really? You don't look like a QB."

"What do I look like, Coach?"

"I'd say you'd make a good tackle."

"What do I look like, Coach?"

"You?" The coach stepped back and looked the next boy up and down. The little mob parted to give the coach a better look. "Fullback, maybe."

"All right!"

"What about me?" said eight voices at once. And so the coach was obligated to go through the entire crowd, one by one, designating their possible position. Although he had seen very few of us do anything physical other than circle him chaotically in the hall, his guess about our possible position very quickly became our individual designated destiny. He thought I might make a guard.

Everything was clear now. And set. "Coach says I'd make a good guard." A judgment that keen and deep was incontrovertible. We spent the rest of the week telling each other and everyone else what position the coach had annointed us with. It was such a relief to know. It still is.

☐ ☐ ☐

Guards don't handle the ball much. But how the hell do you practice being a guard all by yourself? So some evenings Dad and I would run around in the field out back, just making lazy, jogging loops in the ankle-deep grass while we lateraled the ball back and forth incessantly. He would throw it to me at different angles, high, low, in front, in back. "You gotta be ready for anything," he'd say. Sometimes he'd throw the ball on the ground and I'd leap to cover it. "Good!" he said. "It's tempting, like greed, but don't try to pick it up. Just cover it with your body." Sometimes, while we rested on that prickly grass, he'd reminisce about his college days in Scotland playing rugby. "No substitutions or timeouts," he said. I was impressed.

A few weeks later the varsity coach invited a handful of us to attend a varsity practice. Not that we'd actually get to do anything except acquire some horrible morning-after leg pains from suddenly overexercising those limbs. But to be invited, to be involved, even if only watching, was very exciting.

There might have been eight of us. We showed up in the high school locker room immediately after classes; not that we were too eager or anything, but we were inside those smelly cement confines before the 3:00 P.M. bell had stopped vibrating. No one was there. It was the eeriest thing. We milled about, lost. My eager anticipation of practicing with the varsity had been diluted the previous evening when I realized what this also meant; I was going to have to get naked in front of three or four dozen other young males. I had considered riding home right after classes, changing there, and riding back to the practice field, which would preserve my visual chastity and get me on the football field in time to go home for dinner. I had my football gear in a shopping bag and set it down in a far corner of the locker room.

At 3:07 the door burst open and in came three dozen high school boys. They were in their own club, having practiced and suffered together since the broiling days of late August, when the brown grass actually crunched underfoot. We were not part of their team. They had labored through many weeks of hopeful practices, disappointing losses, and a few victories. We had not.

Their talk was foreign to me as they prepared for battle and we prepared to pretend. The coach came in then. He pointed us out as a group, said he had invited us to watch practice this afternoon because we'd be playing for the same school someday, and it was important to learn that practices were more important than the games.

More important than the games? Well, there was about five times as much practice each week as there was game. But I had thought practice was just something you endured in preparation for the glory. There was little time to ponder this because the large boys were turning around on the old wooden benches to look at us. They didn't look so uncomfortable on this Monday, the one day of the week their uniforms and undergear were dry. Theirs was a benign examination of us because we had just been protectively sheathed from ridicule by their god. And ridicule was the worst thing that could happen to you in those days.

The practice went well, I think. After the grueling calisthenics, which went easily for the varsity because they had been doing them for over two months, the team broke up into pieces by position—offensive linemen over here, defensive line and linebackers over there, defensive backs there with the running backs, the quarterback, and the center. They didn't just line up and play each other for two hours. They took the game apart piece by piece, just like Dad had said. Sometimes the linemen practiced just one step, their first after the ball was snapped. Time after time, they'd line up in their starting stance. A coach would call signals and stop; nobody moved. He'd start again and, as one, the four huge guys would take one step forward and slam up on their invisible defensive opponent. Then they'd do the same to the other side. It looked like a complete waste of time.

The backs were walking—walking!—through a new play, time after time in slow motion. One guy kept planting one foot in the wrong place. "Again!" the coach shouted. One foot was wrong? I mean, c'mon, coach. It was cold on the sidelines, not doing anything. We hesitated to pick up a ball and start playing catch, afraid the coach would yell, "Hey, are you boys paying attention over there?" The penalty for being deemed inattentive was to run two laps around the field. "Take two," some coach would say. No one shouted anything derisive, knowing painfully well they could be next.

Of course, none of us was sure what we were paying attention to. But it was very important to appear as if you knew what was going on, one of the single most important lessons learned for a life in business meetings, it turns out. So we stood around in our store-bought football costumes. We were not smart enough yet to be embarrassed because our mothers had washed the outfits specially the previous night so we'd look nice, unable to conceive that there was a place, time, or culture where not looking nice was desperately appropriate. Our arms were akimbo because we had no pants pockets to safely house our hands. And we knew the entire world would notice this. We were bored to death, and we were afraid to show it, having invested so much mutual anticipation in how great this was going to be. Also, we were cold, toe-numbing cold, which is what happens when boredom seeps into your shoes. This was not what I had in mind for football. I wanted to do.

There was some doing in the last twenty-five minutes of practice. The whole team came together for a scrimmage against each other. This was not grade school classmates running around in the park playing keep-away in a game punctuated with laughter and giggles. This was serious, very serious, knock-'em-down-don't-help-'em-up competition among guys who sat at the same cafeteria table together, who intentionally dropped pencils on the floor in study hall to sneak a peek into forbidden places, and who spoke respectfully to almost every teacher. But here they were, face mask to face mask, growling, threatening each other, sweating, swearing, slamming into buddies to prove their mutual mettle. These guys looked very angry and the mud on their cheeks didn't help. The meek might inherit the earth, but they'd never make the football team.

Going up against the hated, faceless demons from Mogadore was one thing. It's easy to believe the worst of people you don't know. The opposition had no respect for anyone. Their uniforms looked mean. They naturally played dirty. They smelled. They won, too often. So knocking them down hard and maybe grinding them a little into the dirt on the way up was okay. But here were our own coaches wanting our guys to do it to our guys. They wanted all friendships suspended. Only the best would play come Friday.

Now, I was intimately familiar with the almost desperate American need to compete. I had spent considerable chunks of childhood in Canada, my parents' home country, where competition was minimized, off the hockey rink anyway. For a long while I had thought that American kindergarten teachers were closet Canadians, so interested were these instructors in keeping the waters placid and smooth. Kindergarten was the last year in school when everyone talked sweetly about how nice it was to share with each other and how really important cooperation was. I didn't really think much about all that sweetness. It made as much sense as anything else then. Two-man sack races were fun anyway. And first graders really aren't in a physical or mental position to challenge anyone past kindergarten anyway. Cooperation was the Gospel, according to Mrs. Dwyer, part of the system of life that we were supposed to soak up. Those were the rules, and the thought of challenging or contradicting them never crossed my mind. In fact, the idea of giving rather than receiving fit perfectly into football's philosophy later.

But life changed abruptly in American first grade. That's when competition began being drilled into us. I was a little uncomfortable with the change; I still am. But it was always somebody against somebody else. Even in spelling bees. Us and them. Boys against the girls. Even numbers versus the odds. This row against that row. Front of the room against the back. This seventh grade against that seventh grade. This school against that school. This town fortress against that one. The bad guys. Over there. Different. Apart.

I never had any problem getting up to compete all-out against the Thems of the world, the faceless, valueless heathen who keep appearing on the horizon of my life like all those endless legions of aliens who methodically march on to the top of the screen in electronic games. They deserved to be vanquished, to lose, or worse. After a hard day of trying to out-think, out-dig, out-question, and out-write reporters from other publications, I still have problems suddenly shucking all my competitive instincts to go share a comradely dinner.

It was combating other members of the Us-es that gave me real difficulty. My competitive urges were strong, very intense, and not susceptible to being turned off or down, not before the end of the contest anyway. Sure, I would shake hands afterwards, not because that was part of the sportsmanship thing, but because the coach said to and he was the boss. Even as I shook my opponent's hand and said, "Good game," I was silently vowing to get even next time. But it was—and is—nearly impossible for me to envision two best friends going out after work to beat each other's brains out on the handball court and then stop off to share a couple of beers afterward.

So it was amazing for me to see these study hall friends

suddenly trying to grind each other into the soggy soil of northeastern Summit County. When the football moved, these guys charged at each other with a violent intensity that frightened me. They pushed and shoved. They groaned and grunted. The linemen struggled upright. The backs ducked into the cracks between sweating bodies. The linebackers rushed up to fill the gaps. The defensive backs flew in to deliver the coup de grace. There was a scuffle or two, even after the whistle. I heard the s-word many times. How could these guys ever speak to each other again, let alone remain friends? Or teammates?

But they could and did. As darkness fell on the field, the coach's whistle blew. "All right," he yelled, "everybody up. Down on one knee." Finally, I'd get at least one part of my uniform dirty. He talked to us then about how good this Friday's enemy was, how much better we would have to practice to have any hopes of success. He saw signs of progress. He didn't want us to think he didn't see those of us who were working hard, trying to improve. But he also didn't want us to think that he didn't see the malingerers either, those guys who thought because they had a good game last week, they could coast this week. "After every game," he said, "you gotta start all over. You gotta want it." He paused. "That's it. See ya tomorrow."

We got up and started to straggle back toward the school. "Hey," every single coach yelled simultaneously. "Run it!" So we reluctantly began to jog, at least until we got around the corner.

□ □ □

The next few years of my life were divided not into months but into two seasons—football, which happened to coincide with fall, and the off-season, which was everything else. Slow-motion baseball, for me, forever disappeared from the face of the earth. Especially after 1954 when Dad and I had tickets to the fifth game of the World Series and the Indians lost the first four.

Football was faster, rougher, more urgent, like violent chess. The running clock added an intriguing complication. Weekly games lifted football from the mud of the mundane. With my eyes, I was obviously not going to be a baseball success. With my height, I was definitely not going to be a basketball success. In that sport it did not matter how hard I tried; there still was a huge gap between the ten-foot basket and the four-foot-ten kid. Football liked size and speed, which I lacked. But it allowed determination, force, and wiliness to compensate. A crack for me to squeeze into.

In order to play football, I had to attend school, which was a very heavy price to pay since my teachers consisted of the most soporific squad of men on the face of the earth. They could numb a mind better than novocaine. My parents had decided that I should attend a private boys college prep school in our town. I was accepted with a handful of other local males. The day the letters of acceptance arrived was a very big day. The school was a very prestigious place and knew it. We were all very lucky to be there. The headmaster said so. I should have known what was coming when I read the dress code: sports coats (wool, of course) and solid-colored ties, preferably in the school's colors, every day, even for Saturday morning classes.

The campus was ersatz New England—meaning it was white and old, very old—and kept close track of a few famous family names from the past, though most seemed to be dead. The school had lots of bricks and tiled roofs, heavily painted radiators that hissed, and teachers who reeked of tradition and favored those brushed leather elbow patches. In chapel, each student was assigned his proper place in wooden pews painted white. Freshmen had what were deemed the worst seats, of course—in the back on the sides. I thought that was great. Seniors had earned the right to sit in what were deemed the best seats—right up front in the middle. I thought those were the worst seats. How could you practice dozing during the headmaster's sermons way up front? This academy also had students who carried bulging briefcases, even freshmen, just like junior insurance salesmen.

The school's sole saving grace in my mind was that it had freshmen football. I was a guard, of course. My best friend Dan was a tackle, right next to me. We gave each other nicknames having to do with our favorite Browns players, hoping that some of the skills and perhaps a fair piece of the glory, too, would rub off. He was Bob (Gain). I was Vince (Costello). Thirty-three years later, he was a general in the Pentagon when I telephoned one day to reconnect after some years. "Who's calling, please?" said the general's aide.

"Vince."

"Vince?"

"Vince."

"Vince who, sir?"

"Just tell him Vince is on the phone."

A very brief pause.

"Hey, Andy! How the hell are you?"

That's what football does in forging friendships.

I would live for each day's practice. I was always among the first on the field, wearing pads still slightly damp with yesterday's sweat. I was so eager to learn everything.

Unfortunately, the coaches did not have much to teach. They were mathematics instructors and, I think, had drawn freshman football duty as other instructors were assigned to monitor study halls, except football duty paid a little better. They had to check with each other in hurried whispers on a lot of decisions. Their football decisions during games did not go too well too often and this was our fault for not executing properly. Of course, the school football team did not do too well at the varsity level either, which was yet another way to imitate the Ivy League. Losing with great consistency did not matter at all, you see, if it involved something as irrelevant to life as a rude sport like football.

To me, losing did not build character any more than cold

showers did. Cold showers taught me that I did not want
to take cold showers. Period. Anyone who talks about how
valuable cold showers are can't afford hot water.

Yes, losing was unavoidable at times, those unfortunate
times having a close connection with the days when we
played public schools from our area of Ohio where football
was a religion and Friday night was the Sabbath. I suspect
the opportunity to thump rich kids was not an insignificant
incentive for those schools' players. Losses could be acceptable on any particular day if you knew in your heart
that you had done your own best. That's what my father
said. My father also said, "Some days, the other guy is just
better than you, no matter how good you are." The idea
was to minimize those days through hard practice and close
observation of the other side's tendencies and weaknesses.

And to use them as opportunities to illuminate and eliminate one more of my own weaknesses. "Turn a minus into
a plus" Dad would suggest constantly. Losses had value as
lessons if you were smart enough to dissect them while they
still stung. At first, I didn't always remember to look for
the one thing never to do again or not at that time or the
thing to do better. But Dad would remind me. "How many
times are you going to fall for pitches low and outside?"
he would ask. That's all he'd say. No berating. Just a question. Pretty soon that was shortened to a code. "Minus to
a plus," he'd say. "Minus to a plus," I'd repeat. And we'd
smile.

The idea of methodically eliminating one mistake after
another from my unlimited repertoire of errors all the way
down the long road of life, even past driver's-license-
sixteen, seemed rather exciting. It offered unlimited potential for self-improvement and made even an uncertain
boy feel in control of his life. Acknowledgment of creeping
up such a ladder of achievement would never come from
anyone else because so few knew I was climbing. The satisfaction had to come from within, where it stayed. Which
was okay; I like keeping secrets. Erasing one chink after

another seemed so useful and satisfying that, after a while, I got to thinking "minus to a plus" even when Dad wasn't around. I still do.

Sometimes, though, drawing mental lessons from mental lapses was harder than at other times. In one Little League game I was told to bunt, not surprising since without my eyeglasses the chance of my connecting for even a single surpassed in odds the likelihood of the Indians ever winning a World Series. Walking to the plate that summer evening, I swung the bat with a frightening fury. Look out, left field. I stepped into the batter's box. I stared down that kid from Twinsburg. And when the hardball came whistling toward me, I stepped around, held the bat steady, and went to tap that hurtling white missile gently down the third-base line. Unfortunately, I was gripping the bat incorrectly. My middle finger was between the wood and the ball. It felt worse than hammering a finger. The ball fell directly in front of the catcher, who threw me out before I was halfway to first.

As I walked back toward the bench, disconsolate, mortified, in throbbing pain, I heard a familiar voice. "That's all right," it said. "Minus to a plus." I'll give you a plus right in the nose, I thought. But I can honestly say that I never made that mistake again. Which was his point. I even remember that game when I go to hammer a nail. One more little victory.

It is fair to say that the freshman football coach and I were never close. Coaches should be wise father figures, understanding but firm, approachable but demanding, knowing but not conceited, above all, trustworthy. The insecure ones try to be despots. The good ones may have been only mediocre players, but as coaches they give off an aura of having been there, of knowing what to do now, and of having confidence that it will work if you just do it their way, for once. Like fathers. This coach, on the other hand, was like the father of some neighbor kid down the street. He was putting in all this time, which was great and all. He certainly knew more than I about the tricks and strategies of football. But, unfortunately, that was still not very much. My coach was very defensive—about what, we were afraid to ask. In fact, we were afraid to ask anything, even about what we didn't know.

Some coaches in my experience are open to player's ideas or suggestions, if only as a measurement of how much the younger people are listening and learning. I know Machiavelli was a football coach, so I'm always eager to see several layers of subterranean significance beneath everything those guys do. But I suspect some coaches go along with players' eager suggestions, knowing full well that they are dumber than the Edsel Ford idea but also knowing that the eager player won't believe the coach. That the kid'll (coaches use a lot of contractions like that) remember a whole lot better if he feels the lessons as well as hears them. I once suggested to a coach during a hurried sideline conference that we call a run around right end because it hadn't worked all day and the defense would not expect us to do it again.

The coach looked in my hopeful face. "Okay," he said.

I took the ball around right end and got drilled by three guys. "I guess," observed the coach, "they aren't as dumb as you thought."

Anyway, to this freshman coach, players' suggestions seemed a challenge. "Shut up," he'd say. "Just listen." As if young men learn nothing by hearing themselves say something stupid.

To be fair, I must say that our relationship was complicated by mathematics: He liked them; I didn't. He was challenged by equations with numbers and letters. They seemed so clear and tidy to him. He taught them. I didn't learn them. My hardly ever getting the right answer was a direct affront to him. He wasn't my classroom teacher; the varsity football coach was. But when I did slip into academic difficulty in two subjects, the freshman coach was appointed my math tutor. I'm sure that made sense to the secretary in the counseling office where this matter of football, of any sport really, was a major distraction from the important business of a school, the formal filling of these young minds through classroom lectures and homework assignments.

Two or three times a week I would meet with the tutor in his apartment for an hour of remedial work. It was excruciating for both of us. I could see the patterns in offensive football plays, in the English language, and even in world history. But the patterns of numbers that could also be letters or round letters with little numbers that squared them and varied according to the speed of the train traveling six hours in the same direction from Point A left me literally speechless. I wouldn't even know what to guess let alone how to calculate. It was like trying to pick up a large glob of mercury; every time you'd get a hand on it, the damned stuff would change shape and slip away. It was frustrating, maddening, and probably a tad frightening. My immature and irregularly disciplined mind would wander and procrastinate at the slightest opportunity. He had one way to teach. I didn't get it. That did not please him. He lost patience. He passed on unfavorable reports, including, I discovered later, false reports of my skipping our sessions. I never understood that either.

On the football field, however, life was something else. I would try anything. Tell me to yell during warm-ups, I'd yell up a storm. Tell me to block my man to the left, I'd do it. Tell me to step into the gap on the defensive line and I was there. I wasn't too sure what to do in that gap except get in the way of the runner or his blockers. My technique was nonexistent. But I'd go for it, like a puppy fetching the stick and eagerly awaiting the head-pats.

We did not have a massive squad. But for whatever reason, I did not get to play all the time. On the sideline, I fumed inside. If I didn't get back in quickly, then I'd, I'd, well, I'd not be back in quickly. I started hanging around the coach for a number of reasons. First, I could overhear what he didn't like about the play of others and avoid repeating those errors. Maybe I could learn what pleased him. And if he happened to turn and see me sooner than he would if I sat on the bench, that might remind him to send me back in sooner. Minus to a plus.

Everywhere he turned, there was No. 24. He'd turn to the left to pace the sideline and there was No. 24 smiling, ready to go. Turn to the right, that same little guy was over there, still smiling. He'd turn to look at the bench and No. 24 would just happen to walk through his line of sight. "What the—"

"Hi, Coach."

"Malcolm, is something wrong?"

"Uh, no, sir. Nothing. I'm great. Just staying loose for when you send me back in. You want me to go in now?"

"No! Relax. Go sit down. Or something."

□ □ □

My memory of that football season is overcast. It seems to have been a black-and-white life of frequent rain showers, occasional downpours, and sunshine when I wasn't around. It was impossible to belong to that social sphere off the field. I was the uncomfortable outsider watching that school's mainstream parade flow by, hearing everyone marvel at the emperor's stunning new wardrobe, and unable to see anything but his nakedness. But when I was inside those stale-smelling pads and helmet, I was at home, at peace among friends. I could be me.

There were moments of frustration; on defense, I knew but one way to rush the opposition, full-speed straight ahead. Finesse was a French word, and I was taking Latin. (Yes, I know they're closely related, but from my ninth-grade perspective, Latin-speakers wore togas and the French favored feathers. Also perfume. And wigs.) So if my straight-ahead charge could be even slightly deflected by the opposing lineman, little Andy would charge himself right on out of the play.

There were moments of pain. I recall X-rays at the health office for a dislocated jaw. But, thank God, my mother stayed outside in the car, and I was able to sufficiently subvert the school's normal bureaucratic process by accidentally routing the nurse's reporting slip to the wrong office so that for two days the coach didn't know I was suspended from practicing for two days.

Then, the slip showed up. "Hey, Malcolm." The coach called me over. "The nurse says you're suspended from practice for two days." He said "suspended" as if he could taste it.

"What?!" I said, incredulous because any injury was obviously ancient history. "May I see that?"

My eyes went right to the date. "Coach," I said a little too instantly. "This suspension expired yesterday." And I ran back out with the guys.

One day there was a scrimmage and my left hand must have gotten stepped on by someone's spikes. I noticed nothing at the time, so it must have been several plays later in the huddle when I noticed that the middle knuckle seemed to be about an inch too high. No, wait, it was skin. What was all that skin doing in the wrong place? I realized then, very calmly at first, that like a piece of sod rolled up, a strip of skin had been torn from the wrist all the way down to the knuckle. I realized it was hurting quite a bit. And bleeding a little. Maybe more. That's when it struck me fully what this meant: If the coach saw that injury, he'd take me out.

So when he came into the huddle during timeouts, my left hand went outside the huddle. When he asked how all the blood got on my left thigh pad, I theorized that someone was bleeding and helpfully looked toward the other team to see if I could assist the coach in spotting the poor victim. Beneath the next pileup, I smeared enough mud all over the back of my left hand to hide everything. And the dirt helped stop the bleeding, too.

In the corner of the showers an hour or so later I washed it all off, which required considerable scrubbing. Then it started to bleed again, all over, as I was dressing.

"Malcolm?" said my math tutor. "When did this happen?"

"Gee, Coach, I don't know for sure." Which was true.

"You better get over to the infirmary. Wait a second. Gentlemen. Gentlemen! Give me your attention, please."

Uh oh. It was too late for him to take me out of the game, but not to make an example of me. He was holding my left hand up before the half-naked, half-dry throng in that steamy space.

"Gentlemen, Malcolm here seems to have suffered an injury of some consequence." A teen's nightmare come to life: Standing naked in front of a crowd that was staring only at the teen and an adult about to make an example of him. How could I make myself wake up from this horrifying reality?

"No, sir. That's okay. It's just a scrape. I—" He yanked my hand back up in the air.

"Boys, this is what I mean about determination and paying a price. Malcolm here gets a painful injury that probably hurt a bit, but he's playing the game so hard that he just throws the pain aside. Congratulations, son. Good work." And he shook my right hand.

In a few days I was appointed the week's captain for the next afternoon game. Mom came to that one. She got a snapshot of me during the coin toss. From across the field I'm the size of a large ant, so you can't see the bandage. I had a pretty good game and, being captain, simply had to be on the field almost the whole time.

Dad helped out, too. When we would run around out back in our field with the football, sometimes he would reach out and knock the ball out of my hands. One moment I'm holding the football, then suddenly Dad is yelling, "Strip it!" And we're both scrambling on the ground for possession. The first time it seemed rather rude to me.

"What's the goal of every defensive player?" he said.

"To get the ball back."

"Right. Why?"

"So you can score."

"And?"

"Uh, so they can't score?"

"Right. Now, how do you get the ball back?"

"Make him punt on fourth down."

"Yes. What would be better?"

"Well, make him punt on third down. But everybody laughs then."

"All right. What's better than forcing a fourth-down kick?"

"Intercepting a pass?"

"Yes. But what else?"

Pause. "A fumble?"

"Almost right."

Almost right? Pause. "I'm sorry. I don't know."

"Don't be sorry. Be smart. Now what would be better than waiting for the other team to fumble? Think!"

Ask him to fumble? Gee, I knew that when Dad did tell me, I would feel very stupid. But I didn't know what the answer was.

"I don't know," I said.

"Make your own good luck," he said. He stood still one second to let that sink in. Then, suddenly, he was yelling.

"STRIP IT!" Like lightning he grabbed the ball out of my hands.

"Strip it?" I said.

"No," he replied, "STRIP IT!"

"You can do that, Dad?"

"Yes. Of course. Why wait for their mistakes?"

"You can just reach out and take it away like that?"

"Sure. Why not?"

I didn't know why not. I didn't know why either. But this seemed to be a major secret unfolding before me. If the offense didn't have a father like mine, they wouldn't know this trick. And I could take the ball away on every single play.

"— — do?" Dad interrupted my daydreaming.

"What?"

"*After* you take the ball away, what do you do?"

"Fall on it!" Ha. That one I knew. Don't try to pick up fumbles.

"Yeah, if it's on the ground you fall on it." He handed me the ball. "Okay, you take the ball away. You're standing there holding it. What do you do?"

In a flash, I knew. I ran. He chased. I ran more. He chased more. I scored. We fell down and laughed.

So there I was maybe a year later, captain for the week, trying to protect a slim lead and gain a rare victory. We're struggling through their offensive line. Being short, I'm peering through the flailing arms and converging hips of two blockers and I spot the handoff to the fullback. He's a large fellow. He was already shaving—well, obviously not that morning—although the roster said he was a freshman. Can I get through these two guys? If so, can I knock down something that big? Can't wait for help? Make my own luck.

All of a sudden, I don't see Mr. Mount Olympus anymore. I spy an oblong ball under his left arm. STRIP IT! STRIP IT! Like lightning, my left hand shoots over and swats the brown leather. It pops free, easy as you please. The blockers are still blocking. Some of my teammates are still struggling to reach the fullback. Some teammates don't know yet who has the ball. Or had the ball. The fullback is still charging, unaware that he's suddenly useless, even with his whiskers and growls. Only I know where the ball is. It's turning over and over, ever so slowly falling toward the mud. Now the quarterback sees it, too. He tries to change direction in the ooze. His feet flail. To me, that ball looks so delicious and beautiful sitting there in the mud. The referee is backing away, aware of an impending crowd. I leap over the guard's shoulder. I land on the ball. The quarterback lands on me. Both teams land on us.

But I'm curled around that baby. It's held so tightly in my gut the referee can't get it out. "Okay, son," he says.

"It's okay. The whistle blew." I open my eyes. I check to be sure. I'm the last one up. Which has the dual advantage of being like Jim Brown and letting the coach see who recovered that ball beneath all that other humanity. Almost formally, I hand the ball to the official. "Recovered by Number 24. Who is that guy?" I chuckle, mostly to myself.

Minus to a plus.

□ □ □

At the end of my first football-playing season we turned in our equipment, and along with it went my enthusiasm for pretty much everything. What was I going to do with myself without football? Without football there was no joy, no light. All was gray. Without football, there was no belonging to the other guys and the delightfully grueling routine of practices, the intense uncertainties of such legalized combat, and the emotional highs of the games. Those emotions, even the low ones, were addictive. So were the silent personal vows to do better next week. The chance to start over every few days, only one step higher, or maybe just a half-step, or maybe even slide backwards and have to struggle back up and feel that warm sense of accomplishment in doing just that. There were concrete lessons learned for the next skirmish. I knew these lessons only involved football. Outdoors, in special uniforms, getting and dispensing bruises, getting back up. Getting even. Dad said all this was good preparation for life. I might sigh, but I'd never contradict him. To me, football was life. How could there be any higher achievement? Certainly there could be nothing else that touched so many parts of my being. And now, finally, after all these years of waiting for something unknown, it had arrived. Or I had.

Exhausting myself at football five and six days a week was such a relief from everything else in my life, a significant sum of which was, in my teenaged opinion, not fun. Football was constructively escapist. After all, boy cannot live by algebra alone. Or at all.

Day by day, I watched the calluses wane from my off-season knuckles. There was a whole long winter to survive and then a spring, which was always nice in the country, of course, but seemed to be growing strangely shorter by the year. And then another interminable Midwestern summer, which was great in June but annually grew soggily wearisome in July and August when nature's thermostat went haywire. By then, of course, I'd be imposing my own one-man training regimen on myself. And another football season would be in sight.

□ □ □

Without football, my life folded back into grays again. The shirts were white, at least in the morning. Their tails seemed to have a stubborn mind of their own and centered on liberating themselves from the confinement of a belt. The tie was tight around the neck and could not, according to the prep school protocol, be loosened outside the locker room. The routine was somnolent—up early, some light chores centering on domestic animals, a ride to school with a senior, more enforced prayers than seemed necessary to survive the standard week. Everything smelled of wet wool. Social studies was interesting. English was exciting. In Latin and algebra, however, I spent most of my time being a fraud, knowing little and hiding the rest. That colored everything and added to the usual insecurities. All I wanted to do was get through one more class without being unmasked.

Most days there was tutoring in Latin and math. And then came sports, which were required in private schools as part of character-building. I had assumed that my emerging passion for football would carry over to pretty much any physical activity, except dancing, of course. I was wrong. At a height of less than five feet, even in thick-soled sneakers, it was clear that basketball was probably not my calling. If any points, even fractional points, were awarded for hitting the rim, then I would have been right up there among the nation's scoring leaders, except for the dribbling difficulties. There was indoor track, which required strong legs and speed. I had the strong legs. And then there was wrestling.

Wrestling required strong legs. Check. Wrestling required upper-body strength. Check. Wrestling required determination. Check. Wrestling required a burning desire to pit yourself against one other determined individual on a stale canvas mat whose manufacture dated from the early Pleistocene era. Wrestling required a physical finesse. Wrestling required swift moves and swift thinking to utilize your leverage and momentum to your advantage and his momentum to his disadvantage. Wrestling required a desire to wear some old-fashioned sleeveless underwear while kneeling in front of a peering crowd. Wrestlers were required to put their head in some kid's armpit, their hand in his crotch, to exchange sweat, and to struggle. For five or six minutes. No timeouts. No substitutions. No mercy. No excuses.

If you lost badly—and I did way too often—you'd end up on your back flailing like a grounded fish while some thug held you down in a confining hug until the referee slammed his hand on the mat and the other kids exulted in your undeniable defeat. You lose, brother. Wrestling was even worse than asking a girl for a date. At least with that rejection you could hang up the phone and just die in private. Defeat in wrestling is very public, usually preceded by coaches, parents, and friends wincing and looking the other way for an instant, as if not seeing the whole loss could preserve some dignity for that poor familiar soul out there. Defeat in wrestling brought a loud whistle, the ref's hand-slam, the opponents' cheers. Then you had to get up in front of everyone, shake the victor's hand, watch the ref raise that same hand in triumph, and then face your own teammates. They probably offered the kind of pro-forma, enforced condolences that hurt more for their insincerity.

Physically, wrestling was utterly exhausting, infinitely

worse than football. I have no idea who invented isometric exercises—pushing in vain, motionless, against an immovable opposing force. But I do know that person was a wrestler. Who else could grasp the physical frustration and exhaustion of struggling to no end for an endless period of time? And then, after the match, being unable to command one or two limbs to move. Well, actually, I could command them, but they were not inclined to obey.

Mentally, wrestling was intimidating—bone-grinding, gut-wrenching, nose-bending intimidation. I was intrigued by the intimidation part. If only you could just do it, like breathe. But I was not intrigued enough to serve the necessary apprenticeship and make the necessary intellectual investments. Study? For sports? Whoever heard of such a thing? Sports were for fun not for perfection.

Every day I would awaken in my bunk bed—top bunk if I'd had a bad day and needed more isolation—and I'd mentally run through the upcoming day's demands. Days of tests in math or Latin were cause for grimace. Days of a wrestling meet were cause for groans and grimaces. I would pull the covers over my head in hopes that daylight would pass me by, just this once. Leaving the bathroom, however, Dad would peer into my room. "Hey!" he'd say. And that was all that was necessary.

To me, those wrestling days define dread. All morning my mind would wander away from class, where I was being steadily unsuccessful, to that afternoon's impending wrestling match, where I anticipated great failure. My stomach felt as if someone had painted it with several coats of menthol, which was so cold that it burned. I made frequent trips to the bathroom. Headaches could appear, not the passing kind but the ones shaped like golf balls that settle in behind your eyes. Eating food at lunch was out of the question, although I moved it around on my plate adequately.

Changing in the locker room took a very long time, hoping against hope that something would happen to interrupt the tragically unfolding events. Maybe a fortuitous earth-quake. Or a life-threatening fire to evacuate the building. Even a fire drill. Anything for an hour's delay. All right, a half hour. But no such luck. I was inevitably the last to emerge for warm-ups; I wanted no one left in the locker room to hear me vomiting into the toilet, the kind of nervous, dry heaves that produce only yellow acid. The waiting by the mat was thoroughly unpleasant. By the time of my match, I was exhausted. After all that, anything was better, even a humiliating defeat. Just get it over with. The physical relief afterward was wonderful.

There was no solace anywhere. No team to speak of. And since I had purposely not told my parents about the meet, I did not have to report my inevitable defeat. Unless over dinner Dad happened to ask about wrestling that day. "I lost," I said.

"Well, you'll do better next time," he'd say.

No, I won't, I'd think. But, of course, I dare not reveal that kind of attitude to him. "You can do anything you have to do," he was fond of saying. I didn't know enough then to believe; I just accepted his philosophy. Except as it pertained to wrestling, which, I decided, was the one thing I didn't have to do. Along with algebra and Latin.

Losing a well-fought contest has never bothered me for long. But I was very deeply ashamed of being so thoroughly defeated in spirit beforehand. I still am. This is very hard to write. I jump at any excuse to interrupt the memories of that winter. Daily, I was meeting defeat in the classroom. Now, here I was doing the same in athletics. Recreation was supposed to be fun, to re-create a whole, balanced life after the stormy routines of daily life. Instead, I was re-creating defeat after defeat, drifting from disappointment to disappointment. This emotional agony went on, heightened two or three times a week by having a meet. Then one Tuesday I snapped.

As usual, I hid beneath the covers. "Hey!" said Dad. I picked at my breakfast, mentally dallied during class, was late for lunch, distracted in tutoring. I was slow in the locker room, vomited in the bathroom, and appeared in the wrestling room in my usual ashen pallor. I mentally writhed through the endless matches of the lower weights. And then as I rose to prepare for my match, the coach called me over.

"I've decided to have Ted wrestle today," he said.

I was simultaneously stunned and delighted. How dare you! I said to myself. Thank God! I also thought. "You mean Ted is wrestling 148?" I asked in disbelief.

"Yes."

I was furious and relieved. Furious that he had put me through all that intense discomfort and relieved that I would not need to face personal annihilation again that day. Of course, substituting Ted, or anyone, for me made eminent sense if the coach was truly interested in having any chance of winning that weight class. I, no doubt, would have ended up on the bottom again, being physically manhandled by someone of equal or lesser strength but superior wrestling savvy. With a weak repertoire of moves, I would have no idea what to do or to try and so, eventually, would give in to frustration. I'd try to out-muscle him at some point, and if he was quick or just a little smart, he'd move an arm and, Bam! I'd be on my back again like an upended turtle.

On the other hand, not trying also meant not losing, for once. I savored the relief, though I could not show it. It was like recovering from the flu in an instant. One moment the all-powerful nausea, the next a serene sense of well-being for at least two hours, until it was time not to confront my math homework once more. At home, I described the afternoon in some detail. Since I wasn't going to be wrestling anyway, I said, now was a good time to have that postponed surgery done on my foot. It had been out of the question—mine anyway—to do it during football. But doing it now would allow plenty of time for healing before summer and the next football season. The logic was inescapable. Even my parents agreed, after exchanging silent looks.

I had no idea that cutting into the bottom of a foot could be so excruciating. But the pain was eased considerably when I saw the coach spot my crutch.

□   □   □

Track season arrived with my mother's daffodils. Like wrestling, track had a team. But it was also really one of those individual sports that was so intimidating to me then. I went out for track and it brought out familiar feelings. What I did best—that is, get over there from here anyway I could—was not highly prized in that sport. Powerful legs meant nothing in spring unless they produced speed. The willingness to run into people, to fill up a defensive gap with my own body, mattered naught. The powers of observation, to spot something revealing even in the placement of an opponent's foot just before the ball was snapped, gained nothing. And I was not fast. But I was determined.

Running a lot every afternoon would at least help me stay in shape for the fall. And since I was an unlikely candidate to break the four-minute mile, I also got into the shotput, pushing eight-pound iron balls into the air. With typical plodding persistence, I took a shotput home for further practice. I walked around our property, boosting the wad of iron as far as I could, measuring off the rough distance to the definite depression it made maybe thirty feet away, and then oomphing it again in some other direction. My father once suggested that if I practiced enough like that at home, over time our entire property would eventually be lowered by four inches or more.

But he liked seeing me work hard at something that required physical and mental preparation and conditioning. I knew this because he praised me so effusively. Or he did something as simple as lavish a little extra attention on my efforts, which was like the little lab mouse learning that pushing the red button caused the food chute to disgorge a sugar cube.

Out of the corner of my eye, oomphing the battered steel shotput from one new pothole to the next, I would see Dad step outside the door or stand inside a large picture window and watch me for a few moments. I worked hardest at those times, without letting on I saw him seeing me. Sometimes he would stroll out to the field. "How's it going?"

If I said "Great!," then I was getting over confident. If I said nothing, that meant not too well. Without any further words, he'd just pitch in to measure some of my throws and add those measurements to my pad in his tight, precise numerical script. The pad was his idea. "That way," he said, "you'll be able to see your progress at a glance even when it's small." Of course, progress pads became an important part of my life. As I write this book, I keep a pad at hand showing the daily progress in words. I do it without thinking.

I suppose Dad, ever the optimist, hoped that someday the same kind of diligence would spill over from athletics to academics, though he never tried to drive the point home so bluntly. It was a good thing he was a very patient person; people who are good with numbers often seem to have that quality. He would come to the door to greet me after these weekend workouts. "How'd it go?" he'd say.

"Okay, I guess."

"Can I see the pad?"

"Oh, yeah. Sure. Here."

And out of the corner of my eye I'd watch him scan the lines while I hung up my coat; Mom did not permit clothing thrown around.

"You did all right in the beginning. And there's a couple of nice throws at the end."

"Oh, yeah? Thanks." If he said so, it was so.

"What was the trouble in the middle?"

"I don't know, Dad. Maybe I wasn't concentrating

enough." Dad, the engineer, liked concentration. Also planning ahead. Think things through. Everything. Not just in sports. Don't just do, Think. What were all the possible consequences of each step in a daily life? From wearing this light a shirt on this cold a day to pulling away from the curb without looking in every mirror, to not having an umbrella beneath the front seat, to watching where your feet were going on most every step. In football, the application seemed clear. It's second down and seven yards to go for them. What would I do in their place? What had they done in similar spots earlier in the game? If it's our ball in the same position, what should we do? What would they expect us to do? How could we do something that looked like what they expected but would really be something else?

No one would ever remember to do all this all the time. That didn't matter. Baseball players become stars going one for three at the plate. It was the trying and the attentiveness to detail that mattered. Did I know that Jim Hegan, the Indians catcher, studied every batter the team would face all season and memorized the weak spots of each so he could call for that pitch? And Paul Brown took movies of opposing teams to show over and over to the Browns.

Preparation now prevented mistakes later, even preparation at age fourteen. At that age, I thought I was Aristotle to think as far ahead as next Thursday. But someday, Dad said, I'd be twenty-one or twenty-four or maybe even as old as thirty, if I could imagine anything so advanced. And then I'd have my own children to teach. Me with children! Ha! Preparation wouldn't always pay off today. Maybe not tomorrow, or not even next week. But eventually, it would put me ahead of the competition somehow, he said. It seemed to me that everything in life was preparation for something else. What else, I had no idea. But it was important to be ready.

"Always take the extra step," he'd say, which is why one

day I would go on to earn a master's degree when no possible job required it. "If the coach says to run one lap," Dad said, "then you do two."

"What if I'm too tired to do the extra lap?"

"You won't be after a while because you'll be in better shape. Always do the little bit extra, it'll pay off."

On my best shotputting days I was mediocre. (Yes, Dad, I know without the extra practice I'd probably have been worse.) Before most track meets I still had to tiptoe back into the locker room to visit the bathroom just before the competition began. But I was trying. (Very trying, my mother would have added.)

One day someone else got sick and the coach said he wanted me to run the 440-yard dash, which is a dash only if you're watching from the stands. From the track, it's a fast marathon. "Coach," I said, in case he hadn't noticed, "I'm not very fast."

Fortunately, for my fragile ego, he did not say, "I know."

Instead, he said, "Don't worry. Will and their guy will battle it out up front. You just go for third. We need those third-place points."

I was shocked. In a way, it was pleasant; he seemed to have the confidence in me that I could help the team in a spot role. That felt good. But the idea of settling for third seemed strange to me. It flew in the face of everything my father had taught me. "Always do your best," he'd say. "You can do anything you have to do." "Never give up." The fact that I had given up so consistently during wrestling was part of that individual sport's pain and my shame. And to whom could I ever confide this? Clearly, my worst efforts had earned last place in wrestling. But it had never occurred to me that my best would not be first. Now, here was my main in-school, after-class authority figure, a man who knew what he was doing, even if he did wear shorts in April, and he was telling me to take third. Coaches were like dads; you had to do what they said. They knew. They spoke the truth.

He didn't think I could take first place? The nerve. Secretly, I determined to go out on that loose track and beat not only the other team but Will, too. How could I possibly get in trouble for doing better than coach wanted? I'd stay close to the two leaders all through the lone lap and then, just before the end, I'd summon up my best fourth-quarter courage. I'd slip in ahead of both of them. I would actually win the race. Let those other two guys battle it out for third place. And the coach, in awe, would slap me on the back and say, "*Nice* job, Malcolm! Nice job." Even Will would be impressed.

The gun went off and the crowd of would-be men sped down those cinders. No one behind me mattered. I was flying. My arms were pumping properly. For once, I was not throwing my head all around, panting. I was puffing in stride. I stayed close to those notorious speedsters. We came around the fourth turn. I turned it on. They tried to, too. I pulled out all the stops, reached down inside myself, and ran faster than I ever had before.

I took third.

No one said a thing. Not the team. Not the coach. I walked around the infield ostentatiously puffing, giving everyone plenty of opportunities. I saw Mom heading for the parking lot. My finish helped the team. Good. Fine. But there was, I determined, absolutely no satisfaction in finishing third. How could anyone, especially the only son of two only-children, be happy with third? Even if he did have fifth-place speed.

That spring sports season ended with an intrateam competition. Since I hadn't acquired enough points for the team in competition with other schools, the only way I could qualify for the team picnic was to run 220 yards in 27.5 seconds. That seemed very important at the time. According to my progress pad, I had never run it faster than 28.

On the last day of qualification I warmed up early. I was first in line to try. The gun went off. I tore down the straightaway.

28.0.

Okay. No problem. Plenty of time to try some more. That's the advantage of planning ahead. More time for extra efforts. I walked around the track. Okay, I was ready again.

Bang! Puff-puff.

27.8.

All right. That's progress.

Ready, again. Bang!

28.3.

28.3? There must be some mistake. Worse? How could I do worse? Of course, I did not share my approaching panic with anyone. The others were busy running their own qualifications. And making it. The picnic prospect was slipping away.

So was the afternoon. The coach looked up from his weathered wooden clipboard. "Malcolm?" he said, surprised. "Are you going again?"

"Yes," I said without moving one tooth.

Bang!

28.

Goddammit! Why wasn't I ever good enough? Why was 220 yards so far? When you said an eighth of a mile, it sounded like a hop, skip, and a jump. But 220 yards? A half a second? Well, who cared about some stupid picnic anyway? I'd rather be at home reading some nice, relaxing book about the devastation of World War II.

There was time for one more try. After sprints totaling half a mile, I was tired. What was the point? Oh, but wait. Wait one minute. I had told Dad about the qualifications. How could I tell him I gave up without taking my last chance?

I couldn't, that's how. I'd have to run it again.

Well, I'd just run it out. Not really try. What was the point? Naturally, I took the next step mentally. He'd ask what my times were. I'd say, 28, 27.8, 28.3, 28, and 34 or something. And he would see in my eyes the dishonesty in that last effort. So my last bid for the picnic, which I certainly didn't care about anymore, had to be my best.

"Did you do your best?" he'd ask after every defeat.

"Yes," I'd say.

"Well then, there's nothing to be ashamed of." Even after victory, the question was the same. "But did you do your best?" So that was obviously very important.

Okay, I'll try one more time, one more leg-pumping, eye-squinting, teeth-clenching bid to break the 27.5 barrier. Or die trying—whatever that meant.

Bang! A good start out of the block. Legs stretching. Toes pushing. Arms swinging. Lungs gulping. I heard no sound, not even the soft crunch of my track spikes in the gravel. Most everyone else was ready to hit the showers. They were gathered around the coach at the finish line waiting for Malcolm the tortoise to waddle over. I'd show them. I'd set a new personal land-speed record. I thought my thighs were going to explode. And my chest. Where had all that good spring air gone? I tried so hard. I really did.

I blew across the finish line, alone, as usual. I stumbled. I gasped for air. Well, whatever the time, my conscience was clear. I had truly done my best. I headed toward the coach, who was heading toward the showers.

"27.4," he said.

27.4?

27.4! I did it. I did it! Not only was it my best ever, it was good enough to go to the picnic. I cackled to myself. Dad was right, as usual. A good lesson. Wait'll I tell him. 27.4. How about that? Doing my best did pay off after all. I forgot all the pain, the frustration.

"Hey, Malcolm."

I whirled. It was Bruce. One of my buddies. He was running to catch up and congratulate me.

"You didn't make 27.5," he said, smiling.

"Yes, I did," I said. "Coach said 27.4."

"No," said Bruce. "I was standing right there. It was 27.7. Coach said, 'Let's give it to him.' "

And Bruce ran on ahead, feeling pretty good. "Nice try," he said.

I stood there a minute. The coach went by. He didn't look at me. I showered in silence. I went home. Dad was there.

"How'd it go?"

"I qualified for the picnic."

"You do your best?"

"Yes, sir."

"Good. Good. Congratulations."

"Thanks."

On my progress pad I wrote down my new fastest time— 27.7.

□ □ □

The next year I became a boarding student at a different private school. I had gone there for several summers of camp. I liked the military aspect. I liked the structure; it was tough, very tough, but also comforting because the boundaries of behavior were very specific and very quickly came to seem reasonable. I liked the rural campus. Athletics were not optional there. Neither was discipline. Ideally, it was self-discipline, but if you were unable to provide discipline yourself, there were plenty of cadet officers to point out opportunities to study and behave within proper bounds.

It was a boy's school in those days, except for nine faculty daughters. So there were only nine distractions among 860 boys. The faculty was virtually all male, which meant they had once been boys, which meant they knew all the tricks of mischief, procrastination, and teenage tomfoolery. It was like growing up in a huge family of coaches. Coaches for football, wrestling, and baseball; coaches for English, French, and geometry. They were powerful men, these people we called "Sir." When they entered the classroom, we rose, as a sign of respect for their academic achievement and position. And, in return-respect for what we might become, they called us "Mister."

They were firm men but not imperious. They were capable of tough demands and tough punishment. Lying, cheating, and thieving inevitably lead to expulsion if the student court returned a guilty verdict; there was no room for such crimes in that society. Misdemeanors drew lesser punishments, perhaps confinement to campus or loss of certain privileges. Repeat offenders could be required to march around in a circle for a few hours in a mind-numbing pattern that discouraged recidivism. The scales of justice were swift and clearly spelled out. There were no threats, just promises. There were so many healthy activities that were acceptable and a few that weren't. Do them and you are in trouble with us, not with your distant parents. You're on your own. You may ameliorate the penalty by clearly admitting the wrong and facing the consequences. But there will be consequences.

Although this was not the way society at large would act in our adulthoods, the certainty of punishment back then was comforting in a way, like the borders on a path nudging everyone back within the proper, although broad, bands of acceptability. And I found myself carrying and applying those values many years later, even when no one was watching.

I think that school also gave my parents the sense that their frustrated ranks had been bolstered by some professional parents who were blessedly free of emotional involvement in past defeats or defiances. The school staff seemed to sense that mischievious boys do not grow into decent men by threats alone. There was a precise and predictable order of discipline beginning with reasonable requests and then escalating through firm requests, orders, and stern orders, followed, if necessary, by appropriate levels of punishment for misbehavior and equally escalating

levels of praise for appropriate behavior and productivity
in learning. These coaches for life, academic, athletic, and
social, were also capable of extracurricular attention, of
placing understanding arms on some slumping shoulders
while whispering encouragement or a pertinent lesson into
an empty ear. They were more like bosses who care, another of this planet's endangered species.

But best of all, there was football, organized, knock-'em-
down-pick-yourself-up football. I must admit to launching
my share of dart-looks at the backs of these men who dared
to suggest in public that I was cheating on the depth of my
push-ups or taking it easy during the short wind sprints they
loved to assign as unpleasant punctuation for the afternoon's workout. "Well, that's enough of me talking and
you not listening," the coach would say. "Let's do some
sprints."

A communal groan emerged from the suddenly attentive
throng of teen minds.

"What was that?" said the coach. "Did I hear some
groans?"

That sound instantly dissipated. No. No groans anywhere
in our sight. But it was too late.

"Yes," said the coach. "I think I did. And, boys, you
know what that means."

I didn't know what that meant.

"Sir?" I said, raising my hand.

"Yes, Mr. Malcolm." The coach's eyes turned on me, as
did those of my would-be teammates. I sensed danger. But
there was no immediate exit, except straight ahead.

"Sir," I said, my voice trailing off weakly. "I don't know
what that means."

More groans.

"Ah-ha," said the coach. "They *were* groans."

The older boys were already getting into position. "Give
me twenty extra push-ups, gentlemen." We did. Then we
did extra wind sprints, forty yards down the field at top
speed. A brief pause. Then forty yards back at top speed.

Back and forth and back and forth. The top speed was soon getting a little less top. But we had to show real determination, or at least adequately mask our nondetermination, because anyone deemed a laggard was afforded the undeniable opportunity of running around the entire football field once or twice.

"You'll thank me some fourth quarter," he explained. Whatever the hell that meant. If the coach wanted to promote a little team togetherness, he would sentence everyone to run several extra field laps because one team member was loafing during the wind sprints. If anyone dared to criticize that alleged laggard, then we all got to run four extra laps.

"Gentlemen," the coach reminded us, "we all win together. And we all lose together. Does anyone have a problem with that?"

And you know what? No one had a problem with that.

Using shared adversity to forge camaraderie is a concept not confined to football. For generations, the United States Marines, for instance, have employed the mutual suffering of grueling boot camps as the epoxy of their esprit. Freshmen at my school in those days were forced to exist in a slightly lower social caste called plebes. As an only son who had played college rugby, my father had told me of the delights of belonging to a team and sharing experiences with a varied assortment of souls drawn together by their love of the same sport. As his only son, I had difficulty at first imagining any value in belonging to a unit larger than a family. To me, more members meant smaller portions of whatever was being shared.

Until football. The sense of inclusion on a real team was one of the headiest feelings I had ever experienced. It was like being swept up by some elemental and immensely powerful, but friendly, force, better even than Dad had said. The football team was a vibrant, living society united by sweat and common emotions, mutually exultant in victory and supported by shared sadness in defeat. The best of

teams developed their own precarious chemistry, their own
floating and topical sense of humor, their own language and
codes, signals, even facial expressions or hand motions full
of secret meanings comprehensible only by the initiated.

I'm sure this same team chemistry reigns in many sports.
For me, however, it was football, whether it was in actual
games or the longer practices that consumed so much more
time than the official contests. On the good days we were
like a well-oiled machine, each separate part strong and
alert, fitting perfectly (well, near perfectly anyway) with
the other pieces, turning the unexpected into the routine.
On the worst days, little went right, stumbles and fumbles
fouled by inattentions and epithets and further fertilized by
frustrations and fears.

We started with the basics. It was exciting. Everything,
every little move and the big ones, too, were new. The
system numbering the backs and the holes on the line—
odds for the spaces between players on the left, evens working out past the right end. The quarterback was number
one, the halfbacks two and three, and the fullback was four.
The 24-dive was the two back through the four hole. We
drilled play after play over and over again until all eleven
people each had their role down pat, for that day anyway.
Then the same thing to the other side. Then a variation of
that, faking to the two-back and actually giving it to the
four-back through the same hole. And then the fake to
both backs and a light little pass over the heads of the
onrushing defenders to the right end drifting past them.

"No! No! No! No! No!" said the coach. "Don't get rid
of the ball so fast. What's your hurry?"

What's our hurry? Our hurry was to get these fakes over
with as quickly as possible and get the ball to the tall guy
on the right to get our touchdown right away in case the
refs hadn't brought along enough points or something. That
was obvious even to us freshmen. Speed was very important. Always speed.

"What kind of fake is that?' said the coach. Coaches love

to coach with questions; *they* come equipped with an inexhaustible supply of question marks. "Who are you gonna fool moving that fast? Boom. Boom. Pass. Did you see the fake, Neumann? Hello! Mr. Neumann? Would you like to join our practice before taking an extra lap on the way to the showers?"

"Sorry, sir."

Wrong move. Coaches don't really want answers to their question marks. Maybe the slightest nod of a helmet or a lowering of the head in abject shame. But they don't want any answers.

"Don't be sorry! Be quiet! And pay attention. I'm not talking for my health out here." His head looked around at every member of the suddenly keenly attentive squad. "Would everyone like to run a few extra laps tonight?"

Every time I see one of those time machine movies I fantasize about going back to my high school football days to just such a scene at just such a practice. And when the coach asks that last question, I would eagerly pipe up, "Oh, yes, sir!"

I have never really seen an exploding coach.

□   □   □

Every day we had reviews of the past plays and added a few new ones. Every day the defense drilled on countering the same things. Every day we did the same basic drills and exercises. Every day I couldn't wait to don my still-damp pads and get out there where nothing mattered but the now and the doing. I could do no wrong in football, especially on defense playing linebacker. Actually, I did a lot that was wrong, but the way the coaches handled it in practice, the mistakes became more of an opportunity to improve, not further proof of my inadequacies.

Sure, there was a fair amount of yelling, in the usual coach's question format. "MALCOLM! WHAT THE HELL ARE YOU DOING WAITING WAY BACK THERE? DON'T YOU SEE WHERE THE BALL IS?

GO TO THE BALL, SON. HIT HIM BEHIND THE
LINE. DON'T GIVE UP A FIVE-YARD GAIN LIKE
THAT! NOW, C'MON. LET'S START THINKING
HERE, OKAY?"

Gulp. With the underwhelming wisdom of a fifteen-year-
old, I thought I knew what happened to people who stepped
in front of large vehicles moving at high rates of speed. I
was scared. But, all right, if the coach wanted me to step
up into the hole, I would. The next time I saw their guard
block one way and their tackle block the other, I ran right
up and filled the hole. KA-BLAM! I got run over by one
or two trucks coming through. I didn't really see how many
there were. I was uncertain for a few foggy moments exactly
where I was.

Where I was, of course, was on the ground, sitting, getting my bearings as the others unpiled from the chain reaction collision I had ignited. I did mess up their play. Not
much glamour in that corner of football, just a dose of
childish courage and, most importantly, a gesture of teamwork; I do this to enable you to do that. I did take out one
of their blockers, I think. To this day, I don't know who
made the actual tackle. I think the coach said, "Good job."
I'm not sure. He said something "job."

But more importantly, it was yet another notch in an
accumulating collection of experiences that lead me to an
inexorable conclusion: I *can* do many things that I never
thought I could do. It takes steady reminders, recalling
some football incident from the memory bank and remembering its unlikely outcome because I had tried harder than
I knew I could. That pattern has never stopped accumulating since then.

The next time that hole appeared in our line, I didn't
have to think. I ran right up there full steam. And this time
I didn't stop and wait. This time I kept on going to keep
my momentum. This time I ran into him. They took a two-
yard loss on the play. I did it! I did it! Heh-heh. Who said
little people need help?

Some of the coach's criticism was more pointed and frustrated. It might even verge on abusive by today's standards. But it never occurred to me to complain or talk back. I hated these men for it. But it never occurred to me that their complaints, their mocking questions or suggestions weren't directed at improving my play. I felt good that they were investing so much attention in my doings, even in the melee that was a football play and the grandiose chaos that was a living, breathing football game. These were The Coaches. They got respect whether I wanted to give it or not. Dad had made that clear. And I knew that these men really cared, that they saw secret things in me that I did not discern, that they knew the secrets to unlocking the full joys of football within me. If only I worked hard enough.

There was always so much to think about, so many places to look for so many little things. So many balls to juggle in so little time. If you weren't constantly compiling new tactics, the enemy would sense your vulnerability. They'd set you up with what looked like a run between guard and tackle, and when I ran up into the hole, oh-oh, no one there had the ball. I caught a glimpse of that brown object lofting over my head to an end strolling through the territory I had just vacated. Damn!

That was the hardest part, tempering my gung-ho enthusiasm to try the latest moves I had just learned. Always rushing in, and not always being right. Thinking. "Andy," my father would say patiently, "Just stop and think a moment."

The coach put it somewhat differently: "THINK! DAMNIT, MALCOLM. THINK! Third and seven. They're not likely coming up the middle, are they?"

I was smart enough not to answer. File that one away. Always know where we are on the field. Always remember that all these little things always add up to something larger. So many details to keep track of. And plan ahead. I had a hard enough time regaining my breath after each play, but now there was something else to do. Check the down markers. Which wasn't easy without my glasses. But so what? This wasn't grade school gym class. It was no longer acceptable to list difficulty as a reason for not completing an assigned task.

And then a funny thing began to happen off the field, too. My homework was always done. My in-class attention span was somewhat longer. Little daily things were more important off the field, too, because they all added up. Life in general seemed in sharper focus. My grades improved. "Do you suppose," my father asked my counselor, "we could arrange for Andy to play football year-round?"

That would have been just fine with me. The sense of firmly belonging to a larger unit that really wanted me was a powerful force. Suddenly I had all these older brothers who liked me, or at least accepted me. We suffered with each other. We exulted with each other. We protected each other. We exchanged knowing nods of recognition off the athletic field, visual confirmation of our silent bond. We built up a battery of stories to exchange and reexchange over time as verbal confirmation of our links.

Like the time early in high school when I was getting muscled by an opposing lineman who was spending more time flinging his elbows and knees about than trying to get through the line. I had caught one of his knees between my legs and returned to the huddle complaining again about this dirty player. "Well," said one of my linemates, exasperated with my continued whining, "what are you going to do about it?"

I was stunned. With my mother several hundred miles away and the other player's presumably at least as distant, it had never occurred to me that anything could be done about this unpleasantness. Though solidly built, I was rather small, like a fireplug. Being towered over by this other guy had seemed like rainy weather, something you ran into often enough and had to accept somehow if you were going to be outdoors.

I began to scrap back, hesitantly at first and then with a

ferociousness that would have been frightening off the field. I didn't wait for him to attack anymore. I blasted off the ball first. I met him on his side of the line, elbows swinging and feet stomping. This had very little to do with the football game under way. It was a test, a teen territorial struggle to determine the day's level of physical intimidation. Who was going to push whom? My effort to mete out physical retribution was a distraction from the actual game at hand. Had the coach noticed or said anything, he would have been critical for putting a personal battle ahead of the team's good.

The confrontation was freshman-frightening because I did not know where it might lead and he was considerably larger than I. But it was intriguing. My teammates seemed to expect some reaction on my part. And they got it, albeit accidentally. On one play this guy's attention was focused beyond me on our quarterback. I caught him under the chin with an elbow. That was about as far up as my properly bent arms could reach. The big guy went down like a sack of potatoes. Lights out.

I walked back to the huddle a little worried inside but strutting nonetheless. The vanquishee becomes vanquisher. Teach you to take beating me for granted. "Jesus," said one of our guys, "what did you do?"

"Well," I replied, "I decided to do something about him." It was mostly bluff, implying a particular plan of action, smooth and decisive, possibly even courageous, which had not really existed in my mind. But it worked— on him and my teammates. Don't fool with Malcolm. Welcome to the real world, kid.

□ □ □

I never got nervous before football games. A brief flutter of butterflies perhaps, waiting in the locker room, dressed and ready but too early. And maybe now and then during the pregame warm-ups when so much team psyching-out is attempted, chanting and growling and doing calisthenics together precisely. "You know," my father had said to me when I once quietly confided my gut-numbing, bowel-flushing fear before a wrestling match, "the other guy is going through exactly the same feelings."

Dad had intended to make me feel normal. It didn't work in those individual sports. It made me wonder why either of us was there. I knew what fear was. Snatching a glimpse across the mat at my opponent, all taut and lean and seemingly eager to begin what I was darkly dreading, I could see no fear there. And when I fell into his grip, I could feel none of his fear either.

But football was different. On game days, I'd wake up early, brimming with anticipation. I'd mentally run down the major checkpoints from the week's practices, at least the ones I could remember. Then I'd drift off into a delicious kind of daydreaming about the heroics I might perform someday, maybe even that day, if only game time would hurry up and arrive. This is now called Positive Visualization. Consultants charge large per diems for teaching it. I called it dreaming.

I loved dreaming. It was so delightfully free of the contradictory realities of everyday life. In my daily routine, alertness, thinking ahead, diligently drawing the details of the day were most prized. There was no time to enjoy the doing, just the having done, efficiently. On the other hand, dreaming, if you could make time for it, had no point beyond the now. Simply enjoy the experience. When I was a little boy, after the morning's chores but before the school bus, I'd often wander back into some nearby woods with my dog. There, while he sniffed around the adjacent roots and guarded our seclusion, I would lie on my back on an old fallen log softened by age and moss. And, to the musical accompaniment of many awakening songbirds celebrating their survival through another night, I'd look up through an opening at the sky and just watch the big puffy clouds drift by on the new day's cleansing winds. I'd think that no one else in the world was watching that one cloud at that moment, which made it mine, though so far away.

Later, during the aeronautical odysseys of my teen dreams, I was almost always wearing my football gear—safe, comfortable, insulating armor. And I wasn't just watching anymore. I was flying. Alone. I'd rise up from within the woods, nicking nary a branch on my ascent. I'd emerge suddenly, shockingly, from the leafy cover of the trees and climb quickly through such a huge openness of sky that I felt really quite small. But now I was in control. I'd twist and turn any which way. Exactly how this was accomplished I did not know and sometimes I'd make a mental note to ask my science teacher how someone like me could loop and soar—there was lots of soaring in these dreams—without a broad flat wing surface to direct the flow of air.

But that was but a vague, idle concern. My primary interest was enjoying the silent flight to nowhere. I would fly in and out of those clouds with a speed that slowed near the top of my immense loops and then rapidly reached startling velocities on the downbound legs that dipped into the clouds or flattened out to skim their tops.

Their surface was not smooth, as they looked from a distance, but marked by lengthy swirls that reached out and flashed by my face as I sped through. Zipping along in the warm air, I might try to grab a handful of cloud. But that soft whiteness blew through my chubby fingers. The only way I could own the clouds was to leave them free to be what they were, white and wild visions that moved on the winds and oversaw all that transpired back below. There seemed no limit to anything in those undiluted days of innocence and colors, not even when I came back down and placed my bare feet, gently, on the floor by my bed.

Classes in these times were no longer hurdles to happiness. They were opportunities to hone my thinking in preparation for the pressures of the upcoming contest. Not that, during some timeout, the ref would demand to know the formula for figuring the area of an isosceles triangle. But that the mental agility in juggling such demanding classroom concepts would spill over to my game-thinking, where quickness, accuracy, and instinct were requisites.

The football seasons merge and mingle in my mind now with disconnected but distinct chapters floating within. The year always began in August with pain and shortness of breath. I would assign myself a physical conditioning program built around sit-ups, push-ups, and running, especially up a long local hill that didn't look that long from Dad's car. By August, the humidity was so intense when I ran that I felt like waving a knife in front of me to help cut it. It didn't seem to bother my dog though, even with her shiny fur coat. She'd pad alongside me leash-free, her pink tongue waving in the air, her eyes looking up at me for approval. The grass was usually burned brown by then, which Dad liked because it meant less mowing. I could feel the brittle blades crunch each time my bent back hit the ground during sit-ups. They would stick to my clammy skin and make me itch. Doing push-ups, my dog took the occasion of my defenselessness to lick my salty face, which I feigned not liking. August, like sunny dawns, was a time of great anticipation. The slate was still clean. The skills presumably one year better.

The football players returned to school a week or so early, according to state practice regulations. We had two workouts a day—9:00 to 11:30 and 3:00 until 5:30—plus evening meetings. By the second morning, the lazy leg muscles, suddenly overworked, ached whenever moved. Most of us tended to walk bowlegged.

We had to run way out to the practice field at the beginning, which was fine, and we had to run all the way back in at the end, which was not fine. We'd break up into the usual groups to practice by position and then merge to slug it out in a grunting practice. They were punctuated by a brief break in the heat for drinks. "Just sip it, boy, sip it," the coach said, according to the health philosophy of that day. "I'll know who gulped it down 'cause we'll all see it coming back up in a few minutes."

Sure enough, within ten minutes two or three players could be seen bent over, their helmets off, retching into the grass. The others pretended not to see them. Then came the dreaded wind sprints—short, sharp dashes that quickly grew exhausting from their repetition. "Let's do a few more," said the coach, who wasn't even panting because he wasn't even running. He was standing there on the forty-yard line exhausting himself saying, "Ready. Set." Then he'd blow the whistle. And off we'd struggle. By the time the next line of players had followed in our tracks, we were to be down in position and ready to return. "Ready, Set." Whistle. Over and over. "You'll thank me some fourth quarter in October," he'd say.

Do these guys all attend the same Windy City School of Cliches?

But, of course, I never said anything, beyond a groan to signal fatigue if he was within hearing. "I can tell who hasn't been working out all summer," he'd announce. "They're the boys who are groaning." Which silenced the ostentatious groans.

"All right, men," he'd say. "Run it in." Which meant quitting time. After that second practice, I'd stand for ten long minutes beneath the cooling shower, luxuriating in the wetness drilling into my scalp. Then I'd hit the water cooler, which due to the liquid demands of thirty-six previously passing mouths, was always considerably behind in its cooling work. But immediately there was dinner, an all-you-can-eat training table in the dining hall with unlimited iced tea, lemonade, or milk, or maybe all three. The warmth of mutual exhaustion was wonderful throughout the rest of the evening, even in the "chalk talks" where the coaches told us what they had told us that afternoon. And there was no thought of post curfew pranks since I was usually asleep long before lights-out.

The season of competition against outsiders began tentatively with scrimmages against other teams. These were, in effect, game rehearsals where the clock was suspended any time either coach wanted two minutes to instruct his charges. The idea was to work on the mechanics of offense and defense against unfamiliar opponents in a setting where first downs didn't matter and no one kept score. Like hell. I kept score—of their points, their first downs on my side, their successful fakes of me, my successful intimidations of them. That's when I learned how loudly actions can speak and how useless bluster and hot air are, at least the hot air emanating from the five-foot-eight level.

If you are over six feet and, say 220 pounds, announcing the devastation you are about to wreak on an opponent may, indeed, give them pause and become self-fulfilling. If you are sixty-eight inches tall and 150 pounds light, making such ominous pronouncements is more likely to give everyone a good laugh. It only took one time for me to learn that lesson. So I opted to become a silencer. It was safer—if I was the deckee, there was no crow to eat. On the other hand, if I was the decker, the violence I delivered could seem magnified by the small package it came from. I'd come flying in from some unexpected direction, trying to utilize every ounce of weight and momentum to my advantage. I used some of those leverage lessons from wrestling. I knew it was not textbook, but I liked to hit some of those lean guys high, especially if they were leaning over a little, which helped me and magnified the impact when we hit the ground, me on top, the opponent in the middle. People tend not to notice how short you are if they are lying horizontal at the time.

I wanted opposing players and coaches to be startled—"Where'd that little guy come from?" I especially liked it when after tackling a back for a loss, I'd hear their coach yelling at his linemen, "All right, damnit, whose man is 45?" That felt good. I imagined people in the stands turning to each other; "Who *is* that No. 45?" I hoped they'd say.

Of course, I never expected to hear any public compliments from my own coach. Public criticism, yes; that might teach many at once. But I had a hard time remembering that I was more often a generic target of teaching opportunity, as we all were. Several criticisms in one day were theoretically helpful for expanding the group's collective wisdom, although definitely dangerous to the individual teen's self-esteem. But public compliments from a coach? Rarely. The best you could hope for was a theoretically approving silence, which was terrific preparation for journalism.

Sometimes the lessons came privately; those were the best. At the time, they seemed to concern only football. The coach would call me over to the sideline to ferry in some instructions. "Tell the tackles to spread out another yard each—they're jamming everybody in the middle to go outside. And tell the ends to stay home—they'll be coming back at them any minute now."

Then, perhaps, the coach would see a harried wave of worry wash over my face beneath the mask. "Hey! C'mere," he'd say. "Relax now. We've got plenty of time. You're gonna worry yourself into some silly mistake out there."

There were a fair number of mistakes. Some I knew the instant they happened. On third and long, I'd still fall for their fake into the line, come charging up, or even take just a step or two toward the middle before catching myself. Oh, no, I'd think. I'd halt. And there went their other back around the outside, just a step or two beyond my reach. I'd have to go charging full speed downfield, and if he wasn't too fast I'd pull him down. And then I'd sneak a peek at our sideline and spot the coach shaking his head.

Sometimes, trying to achieve the perfection I just knew would earn the approval of this father figure with the clipboard, I saw too many of my mistakes. Maybe even more mistakes than there were. I'd see errors, even if coach hadn't. I'd start working too hard, overreacting to every play in an effort to make up for being wrong. Or I'd be muttering to myself at halftime, condemning a stupidity, asking myself why I kept doing it, vowing never to let it happen again. As if saying it would achieve it.

The coach would squat down next to me. He'd look into my face, allow some time for the frazzled teen mind to focus, and then he spoke. "You've got to learn to let go of your mistakes," he'd say. "Or else they'll only cause new ones."

He paused again.

"Now, the first half is history, son. It's done. Forget it. Just go out there now and play the kind of ball I know you can."

Then he nudged my arm with his clipboard, which in man-talk means, "I like you, but you know I can't say it."

Being at a boarding school, I did not expect my father to be at every game, though he made most of the big ones. I knew he genuinely liked me playing football because he was so interested in my reports after each contest, even by telephone. Not that teens need their parents, or anything. Just that they need to know their parents are still there if they ever do need them, which, of course, they don't. But just in case, you know.

I'd give him the outcome first, then the score, then a verbal replay of the highlights, not necessarily in chronological order. There was always a chunk of regrets somewhere—things not done or not done correctly or well enough. Dad called them "if onlys." If only I'd started one step sooner. If only I'd raised my arm a moment earlier. If only I'd remembered to check the down marker that time. If only that one pass had been caught.

After a few minutes Mom would say she was getting off the line now. Dad shared my joy at the victories and, after Mom left, my disappointment with the defeats. I could almost predict when he would say "Minus to a plus." Take at least one lesson away from each defeat and eventually the defeats will begin to dwindle. Not coincidentally, although I didn't realize it back then, that approach inevitably also helped ease the immediate pain of the loss, especially if it came in a close game decided right near the end.

"Life," Dad said "is full of fourth quarters." I didn't understand him at first. I thought he was talking about money. And my father, the plain-spoken prairie boy, had never been particularly Delphic in his pronouncements. Now I'm a father several times over, and I can't stop seeing all the meanings buried in those six words.

□   □   □

After my first couple of years at that school, football changed for me. One day during offensive drills, as an apparent spur-of-the-moment decision, the coach said, "Malcolm. Go in as fullback."

I looked around for the other Malcolm he was talking to. "Me, sir?"

He looked at me. Then he motioned toward the huddle. He did not yell at my slow reaction. So it wasn't spur-of-the-moment after all. Puzzled, I trotted into the huddle. They had to accept me as a running back; coach had ordered it. But I was uncomfortable. I had dreamed of a lot of things about football—knocking ballcarriers silly, stripping them of the ball, leaping high to tip the pass into my greedy hands with the stubby fingers, running down the sideline like lightning—well, no, like a short freight train—to score a game-winning touchdown. But all of that occurred on defense with me doing the unexpected, with me appearing from out of nowhere to turn their long pass into our interception. Minus to a plus. And if I dropped the interception, then it was still a plus because I had broken up their pass. A no-lose situation for the loner with the self-confidence only as thick as his football pads.

But offense? That involved being in the spotlight. Not as bad as writhing around on a wrestling mat, but close. Most everyone watched the ball all the time; that was another thing that made me different. As a spectator, I was always watching for the little athletic drama away from the ball, the private combat, the hidden trick that made the difference, the real story of each play's success or failure that only that lone player and I would know about (at least until the game films came back).

It was one thing as a young defensive player to daringly dash in to steal the ball and the spotlight. It's quite another to have it handed to you, while everyone steps back to see what you do with it. And offense was so complicated. Defense was the Gang of Eleven. We each had one or two responsibilities to check and then get to the ballcarrier as fast as possible. Basic math. Maximum mayhem. But offense had all those plays, so many of them built to look alike. Each play had eleven pieces, each vitally linked, each hopefully coordinated with the others. When they all clicked together, smoothly, intricately, and exploited an opponent's weakness, oh, my, was that sweet. Rare but sweet.

As a guard, I was but one of those pieces. I had to know what my job was and that of the guy on each side of me. But that was it. If it was a pass, I'd better not go more than one step ahead. If it was a run, those yahoo backs who thought they were gods in jockstraps were on their own. I couldn't worry about them. They could find the hole I made for them or die. Then we could hear them moan in the huddle about the line not working hard enough.

Now and then I'd had enough of them. "You could always open your eyes while running," I'd suggest.

"C'mon, guys. Shut up!" said the quarterback. Which was okay with me since I'd gotten my jab in.

But damn, as the fullback, I'd have to know which way every lineman was going to block his opponent. Which is a lot, I mentally whined. And there wasn't much time to think about all this either. You just had to do it, fluidly. It had to come from a fast scan of a mental checklist, like the answers to fourth-grade flashcards. The quarterback calls the play. That play means I do this. The huddle is breaking up. Now, the guard is going to pull and go left. The tackle is going right. Everyone is getting into position. Then, I'm to hit the gap in between. The line is bending over, putting their knuckles on the ground. Don't get too close to the other backs. Okay, now remember the count. Don't point your feet and give everything away to some eagle-eyed linebacker seeking hints. The quarterback's hands are going under the center. Don't look at where you'll be going— and don't not look either. Look everywhere to disguise everything. The quarterback is barking. The count. Shit! What was the count? Watch the back of the quarterback's ankle. It'll tighten just in time. Now, go!

Where was the fun in an ordeal like that? Put any more thinking into offense and football wouldn't be a game anymore. Of course, it could have been worse. I could have been the quarterback, who had to know everything about everyone in every play and be setting up an overall strategy in his head. I knew I was no quarterback. I knew I was no fullback either. Way too slow. What could be done about that? Nothing. What could the coach have in mind? Who knows? What could I do about any of this? Nuthin'.

No time to care. In the huddle I was switching to survival mode. The coach wouldn't expect too much of me, since my experience at fullback totaled less than one minute. But I still had to do the best I possibly could in case I was asked about it by Dad or my own conscience, which was becoming pretty much the same. The coach would probably give me the ball right away. Why waste time? That's what I'd be expecting if I was still alert on defense.

We all heard the coach give the play to the quarterback. But according to protocol, the orders had to come from the player-leader. He called the play. It was a fake to me into the right side and then a pitch to the halfback going way wide. The coach was a sly fox, he was. Maybe he didn't want me as a running fullback, but as a faking fullback. Maybe this was just part of an Andy assassination plot.

I got killed on the play. It seemed like everybody tackled

me, even the guys on the sideline. The entire defense was dead certain Malcolm would get the call. Without thinking, they all converged on me. I didn't think here was room on my body for so many hands and shoulders. Thud! I almost got to the line.

But I didn't have the ball. Ha ha. The defense was also dead wrong. There went the halfback zipping around right end and heading downfield untouched. A slow-thinking safety, who had missed my fake and subsequent burial, suddenly found himself accidentally in the middle of a would-be touchdown. He caught up with the halfback, but not before we notched a twenty-yard gain.

"Everything is not always what it seems, is it?" The coach aimed the lesson at the defensive end, but he hit everyone over there, especially with his mocking chuckle. Thanks a lot, coach. See if you can get those animals on defense any more riled up so they eat me alive.

Back in the huddle to call the next play. Uh-oh. It was to me, crossbuck right. My stomach jumped. Yet it might be fun. Everyone, including me, was going to be moving left for two counts. Then I'd be coming back to the right.

The quarterback was talking to me. But he was looking at the end. He knew someone on defense was watching his motions for hints. Hell, so was I. He was a clever quarterback. He was a senior. "Okay, Malcolm," he said, "don't forget that means you make a big one-step fake to the left and then come back over Neumann. Got it? On two. On two. Break!"

They were two very long counts. My life went into slow-motion. We lined up, each player spacing himself properly from the next. What would fool me the most if I was watching me from defense? The quarterback was surveying both sides of the line, ostentatiously waving the wingback up closer on the left side, which was relevant to absolutely nothing, but they couldn't know that. So perhaps they'd waste a man or two worrying about him.

The shoulders! That's it! If my shoulders weren't moving

big-time on this upcoming fake, the linebacker wouldn't buy anything anytime. I remembered that from watching TV games. The line was down. So was I. My eyes scanned the line, left to right, eight khaki-clad fannies facing me, and beyond them, portions of mean faces scowling through face masks. They didn't know what was coming. But I did. This offense might be fun, after all. Oops, the count.

Stand up, higher than usual. Let 'em see me. Everybody to the left. One. Two. Now me back to the right. Where's the ball? I don't know. Gotta go. Keep low. Four yards through the line, they begin to hit. Hi, guys. It's me, Andy, your teammate. They don't care. They hit some more. Like a fish feeding frenzy. They were fooled before. Now they are annoyed, at best. But they're hitting the shoulder pads. So we all continue together for some more yards until their combined weight is too much. And down we all go. That was kind of fun. I get up real slow. I know how this running back stuff goes.

I head back to the huddle. "Mr. Malcolm," the coach said. "Where did you learn to run like that?" He said it out loud so everyone could share in the lesson.

Damn! A disaster on my first play. I run down my mental checklist one more time: I had my left arm up for the handoff, my right hand cupped below, shoulders down, head up, eyes open, knees pumping, feet lifting free from flying hands and legs below. What was wrong with that? What had I missed watching the games on TV, then pretending out back in the field. I couldn't think of what I hadn't done.

"I don't know, sir," I said. "Did I miss something?"

He paused.

"No, son. You did fine. Keep it up."

□   □   □

That was the end of my days as an anonymous guard. I still got to play linebacker, which was always the most fun, freelancing for fun wherever the most action was. But now there were countless new challenges as a running back, a whole new discipline and attitude to adopt. New requirements to think about. Fakes to make, fakes to shake. The telltale moves of each position actually complemented each other in my mind. I knew what linebackers were looking for and worried about. I was learning what fullbacks needed to do and think about.

The bare bones of my new regimen came in our playbook. It was a modest publication, twenty to twenty-five pieces of white paper stapled together, each page carrying the diagrams of two offensive plays hand-drawn by the coach on stencils that were fed into the math department's mimeograph machine. Out came endless pieces of white paper with purple ink and a distinctive alcohol smell that I always associated with school tests, until I played football.

With X's and O's and lines, arrows, dashes, and circles, the coach showed us how he wanted each play of our football life to be run. It detailed each player's responsibility on each play, the line of every blocker's attack, where each fake was to occur, and the route that the ball would actually take. This was, of course, the idealized version of life that we could shoot for; if we performed our individual assignments all together, this good thing would happen, hopefully, and the reward might be some points for our side.

To some kids, this playbook was one more teacher-produced thing to misplace in the mindless winds of early teen life. To me, this quickly weathered collection of paper was a sacred publication, a sign of the big-time. I studied it at my desk so much that the staple holes grew enlarged, the corners curled, and the margins filled with cramped notes. These were notes that I never read again (these also were notes that no one could ever read again). But the writing-down had burned them into my mind.

On paper, these football plays were just purple squiggles, lifeless and one-dimensional. But in my mind they came to life, in color, full of action and drama. I couldn't stop looking at these pages. They were so full of potential and things to learn. I'd watch each position. I'd imagine the play unfolding. I'd steer one guy this way and then imagine how all the others would react. Then I'd have him go the other way and see what happened, maybe tossing in something unexpected, like a lateral, and then see how everyone would react. Maybe they got a long gain or a touchdown out of that trick because in this mental chess game the linebacker coming from the far side of the field took too sharp an angle of approach. So I'd rerun the play with the linebacker—okay, I'll be him this time—smartly shifting his approach, giving up five more yards to meet the ball-carrier but, this time, getting him down. The combinations in these games were limitless and never bounded by time. I had never been so fascinated by thinking.

I carried my playbook everywhere inside my three-ring notebook, even after the football season ended. This was for obvious security reasons; an enemy could sneak into my empty room during an absence at class and photograph the entire contents with one of those tiny spy cameras. And having the playbook always at hand enabled me to test myself without warning at any free moment. All right, Andy, on a wing-right 47-pitch, how far back from the line do you loop to give our end time to come back on theirs?

The playbook (actually, it was more of a play-sheaf) was life in a plan, my lasting link to football. The diagrams were just dry symbols on paper. But I was excited by how, on the field, each one could magically come to life in a human drama that rarely unfolded the same way twice. Change the route of just one symbol here and the chemistry of the whole page changed in real life. Let one blocker fail to fulfill his task over there and that turned this player's assignment into a desperate improvisation here, which caused another player to do that and another to forget this and pretty soon what looked so cut and dried on paper became a dramatic cascading calamity.

On the other hand, let one blocker do a bit extra and eight others live up to their assignments, let one fake fool the right person and one defender be inattentive for just a split second and if yesterday's rains hadn't loosened the ground so much that the ballcarrier couldn't make his sharp cut, and the ref who never did like our coach didn't think he saw someone illegally using their hands, then the play that looked so complex and idealized on paper sprang to real life and became a beautiful long-running gain or even a touchdown. That sudden event, silently wished on one side and silently dreaded on the other, provided a euphoric unity for eleven players and their sideline compatriots who had worked so hard so long without fully knowing why. This indescribable ecstasy was always there for ardent pursuit, like love; its delivery came much less often than in dreams, also like love.

As a neophyte fullback, I now had to study the assignments of a new O. Fullbacks in those days didn't have to run fast. Good thing. The only opponent I ever outran was running at me. Some running backs try to avoid getting hit. I tried to avoid avoiding getting hit. I'd look for people to run into, especially those dinky little defensive backs who lay back behind the action thinking they're so quick and smart. I'd break through the line sometimes. There'd be open space to the right and a dwarf safety to the left. He'd come charging up ready to give chase. I'd turn left. Unorthodox, perhaps. But why give him a free shot at my back?

I'd turn straight at him. He's used to handling a falling football or a gangly end looking the other way. Let's see what he does with an oncoming train. I'd bear down on him, steam blasting out of my helmet earholes. He'd be running fullsteam, then he'd slow down a little. Wait a minute. The hunted was becoming the hunter. I'd come right at him, not faster and faster but harder and harder. I'm standing straight up. He's aiming his shoulder for my stomach. At the last second, I bend over.

Suddenly his target—my stomach—is gone. Suddenly there's a bulbous, padded shoulder headed right for his face. Good afternoon. Ka-blam. His head bounces back.

If he slips down, I brush through his arm like a blade of grass. Or my churning knees catch him on the chin. And he's suddenly busy trying to remember his first name.

It was great. I loved it. It *was* better to give than to receive.

"Mr. Malcolm," said the coach, as if he had just thought of something, "the point of this game is to get the ball into the end zone. It is not always necessary to try to knock everyone down on every play." But he said it softly, so I knew it didn't bother him too much.

Still, it might be a good point. So occasionally the defender and I would be bearing down on each other, like two male mountain rams in a Disney wildlife movie. Then, at the last instant, I'd duck aside. He'd go flying through thin air. I had to imagine this, however, as I felt an urgent need to get the hell out of there.

Of course, I often got schnockered. One time I broke through the line. I targeted the safety. He wasn't charging up quite as quickly as he used to, which meant we met a yard or two farther downfield than before. That was a six-foot victory for me. Pay attention to the little things, Dad would say, they add up quicker than you think. Which nobody would ever notice in all that moving chaos, except maybe the coach, who would never say anything about it. Try not to live for other people's compliments, Dad had said. This was an awful lot easier to suggest if you were an adult and not easy to do at any age. But that attitude was basically fine with me since Dad's compliments were the only ones that really mattered then anyway. Except that as I grew up away at school, he wasn't around all that much to present compliments and gently offer oblique criticisms. So I took to bluntly critiquing myself according to the quality index I attributed to him. It was a pretty rigid standard and I rarely measured up.

But now there I was emerging from the male maelstrom of the line combat and there was another safety in my sights. I was really going to—suddenly, there I was flying sideways.

There I was going down very hard. See the cocky fullback get nailed. Moving down the line, the linebacker had got me in his own sights. I'm sure I got up slowly again, but that one was necessary. When the cobwebs cleared and I found out who had hit me, I made an indelible mental note to keep scanning the entire field next time I got through the line. I still do it when I come out of a room or a building door. Don't get so focused on one thing in front. Also, don't forget about that humility business.

I was never into a lot of flaunting in football. Emotional, excited, yes, but not that "We just scored a touchdown on your puny little team" celebrating. There were two practical reasons for this. One, I had noticed from that first attempted football game in the eighth grade that what goes around comes around. One way or another, the other guys were going to get their turn with the ball after every one of our possessions. And as good as we might be on any given day, given the power of emotion in the game of football, on the next day, they could just as well stuff the old pigskin down our throats sideways. Or as my father put it succinctly: Be nice to the people on the way up 'cause you'll see the same folks in the elevator on the way down.

And second, my coach didn't allow "showboating." He came from the Paul Brown school of coaching, where slamming a clipboard down was a sign of weakness. He didn't yell and scream, which we got used to. But at first, his unexpected ferocious calm was very disconcerting. You could make a dumb mistake playing and eventually earn your way back into respectability. But the quickest way to the bench on his team was to get into a fight, throw a helmet in disgust, or argue with teammates. The sentence was simple and, most important, swift. "Sit down," he'd say.

That's all. Amazing in an athletic culture where the obvious emphasis is on brute force, intimidation, and violence and the subtler levels are so invisible to most nonparticipants that those two little words—"Sit down!"—could be so deflating and destructive. They weren't even obscene.

"Sit down!" Like a dog. The wise felon would do just that just then. Within a minute, when the emotion had dissipated somewhat, the coach could be found at the offender's side firmly explaining the infraction.

Coming off the field, the unwise miscreant would respond to the coach's sit-down order by trying to explain his outburst. "But Coach . . ."

"Sit down!" the boss would repeat. Then he'd walk away, which is coach-code for "This exchange is over, and if you don't go sit down this second, you are subject to immediate termination." There were regular, though vague, references at times to how football was preparation for life later, although this was obviously just adult obfuscation because football was life and, to me, later was next week. Adulthood was something that befell you, like arthritis, and removed your eligibility to play.

There were other behavioral misdemeanors, of course. Complaining about referees, for instance. Coach apparently thought they were human beings who, by and large, did the best they could in those emotional tinderboxes that are football fields. There were to be no, repeat, no complaints ever about teammates. Each of them was surely trying as hard as you, and to knock their efforts was to ignite the cancer of dissension. Nor could we celebrate our success too much: "Act like you've been there before, boys." Or gripe about the enemy's play: "Let them take care of their points. You worry about your side of the scoreboard."

Which is not to say there weren't other scores settled during the lifetime of a game—shoving bouts, ongoing grudge matches, private combats, and angry exchanges. There was one big opposing fullback in one game (actually, there was a big opposing fullback in every game, but this one really liked to play, like me) who also played linebacker on defense. It somehow seemed that we ran into each other on every play. He was a tough fellow. It's hard to believe he had a mother ever. Those are the kind of guys who just seem to hatch somewhere. They started shaving around eleven, and whenever they entered the crowded boy's room, space at a urinal magically opened up.

So this large fellow would come rumbling through the line with the ball and I'd try to stop him, which wasn't easy. So we'd gang up on him. And then, for an instant, I'd be lying on top of him, my face mask near his helmet earhole. "Why don't you just stay down this time," I said, "so I won't have to keep knocking you down so easy?'

It wasn't really a question. It wasn't intimidation either. He was doing too well. I was trying to distract him. If I got his mind off what he was supposed to do and on to something extraneous, like a teenage verbal shoving match, maybe he'd forget something on his mental checklist, some play, some move. Maybe he'd be thinking so much about this mouthy middle linebacker five yards away that he'd forget the count and jump early. Maybe he'd point one of his feet accidentally before the snap. Maybe one of our linemen would notice and meet him somewhere sooner than usual. Maybe he'd be so angry, he'd tear my head off next time *I* had the ball. Maybe.

What happened immediately was that he started struggling to get up quickly, in defiance. What I did was take my time getting off him, which made him angrier. He struggled more. I leaned on his leg getting up, maybe his helmet, too. He struggled more. "Get off, damnit." But he wasn't dumb. He wasn't going to get into a shoving match after the whistle and draw an unsportsmanlike conduct penalty. So we exchanged some heated words.

"Prepare to die, you little shit," he said.

"It wasn't me who was eating dirt just now."

"I'm gonna get you." He was walking back to the huddle. If steam was escaping, the refs didn't do anything. If it was building in one place, they did.

"Well, you'll sure know where I am, sonny."

"You sonofabitch!"

"See ya." I turned to my teammates. We laughed loudly.

Mockingly. He stared darts out of their huddle. Maybe he wasn't listening to the next play. Maybe this was working. Maybe this had gone too far. Maybe I was about to die.

Now I was very scared at that moment. I had been very careful not to make any threats I was unprepared to live down to. But maybe he hadn't. Too late to back out now. They were lining up. It looked as if they were going to our left. Their quarterback had looked only over there as he walked to the line. Their tackle had moved out a little, possibly to get a better blocking angle on our lineman. I patted his butt to move out some, too. I looked at their fullback. He glowered back. He hadn't wiped his muddy hands on his pants this time, like he always did when he was going to get the ball.

I smiled at him. He didn't smile back. I beckoned him with my forefinger. The ball was snapped. They were going outside to our left. But first they faked to the fullback coming straight at me. I insulted him; I didn't even touch him. They lost a yard. I was relieved.

Who knows if it helped?

□   □   □

As school seasons came and went, my ambitions for sports continued to spill over into the classroom. I had always thought of them as entirely separate. There were classes from 7:40 A.M. until 3:00 P.M., or later if you hadn't done the homework properly. Then real life began out on the grass that smelled so fresh right after it was cut. At first, the long hours of classes were the payment I made for the two hours of football. I saw those two hours as a joyous freedom, although they were probably more rigorous and disciplined than any other time in my life. My memories of specific sports moments still remain more vivid and pro- fuse than any other part of that life.

But there was a steady accumulation of incidents off the field that began to draw the two together for me. Slowly, I began applying the same kind of intensity in some classes as I did in some games. Homework had become something not to put off indefinitely until I was apprehended, but a necessary exercise, like calisthenics, to prepare for the next day's classroom competitions. Some of it, like the reading, I did with youthful zeal. Other parts, like math, I did like wind sprints; they were unpleasant but necessary for a confined period of time to earn the right to endure, and then, the right not to have to do it ever again.

In that school we had to take at least three full years of math. That's exactly what I took, not one period more. I remember thinking in that last week's preparation for final math exams, "Well, this is the last few minutes of the fourth quarter. Hang in there." I always loved football; I still do. But I swear, as a player the fourth quarter lasted twice as long as any other. I know no mathematical theorems to explain why the final fifteen minutes actually lasted thirty, but it's true. Thanks, coach, for having us in such good shape. When the gun would go off and the contest was over, no matter the score, there was a physical and mental relief. I enjoyed the game. And I enjoyed the relief, as long as there was another game scheduled the next week. I didn't enjoy math, but I had come to enjoy doing it the best I could with the teacher as coach. At a June dance, several days before the year's final grades were announced, my math instructor waltzed by my parents. He smiled. "We made it," he said. I felt good that contest was over, but also good to have done it. As long as logarithms never entered my life again.

This realization was probably more of an evolution in thinking than a revolution, but I date this change from an English teacher's seemingly offhand remark late one Monday morning. "You expressed yourself very well in the game on Saturday," he said.

That school was much like an extended family, with the faculty all living on or near campus and students often spending enlightening evenings in the teachers' private lives and living rooms. So it was not surprising that the teacher had seen the game. But his phrasing puzzled and worried me for a moment.

"This time," I said, "I didn't say anything to any of them."

"No," he replied. "I mean your play expressed yourself very well. You can be quite creative."

Me? Creative? Was he talking to me? I just played football and tried to survive. I looked puzzled.

"Well," he said, patting my shoulder, "you think about it some. There's no one way to play football. It's like writing. No one way to write either."

Writing? How'd he get books into this conversation? We're talking football and suddenly this tall guy is dragging in Joseph Conrad or one of those other bearded guys who wouldn't know a touchback from a safety. I had always enjoyed reading writing. I could control that world and I could go anywhere and do anything in books. But I had always thought that writing was something that just happened when some lonely guy sat by himself in an unfurnished tower, usually at night and always in the rain. Probably the door was locked, too.

I was intrigued by this teacher's comment. Not that I'd ever take up writing, of course. There was likely little money in writing for classrooms; Thomas Wolfe never got a cent out of me. Where else but school did people read short stories? And except for Hemingway, all those writer-guys were dead. So maybe it was a dangerous profession, too. I was intrigued instead because maybe this writing business had some lessons that could be applied to football.

I showed up at the English teacher's house the next Sunday afternoon. The Bears were playing on TV and I'd miss watching some more players' feet in their proper or telltale positions. But this avenue of investigation seemed promising, and no other players were around. So I'd have a head start.

The teacher did not seem surprised to see me standing outside his front door, hat under my arm. "Come in, Andy, come in. We were just watching the Bears."

An English teacher watching football? Not watching opera or reading *The Canterbury Tales* or something else in a foreign language? This guy was amazing! I settled in for the second quarter. He turned off the set! He was more interested in me. Oh, jeez, this was getting a little too serious. I stop by to be taught a few English tips for football or something and he's turning to me, without notes, crossing his legs, and smiling as if I had a delivery for him.

"Now, what's on your mind?"

What's on my mind is I'd like to get out of here right now.

"Oh. Well. Um. Nothing really, sir. I just—how's your family, sir?"

"Fine. Just fine, Andy."

"Good. Good. That's really good." My God, his clock was a loud ticker. "Your dog looks sleepy."

The teacher nods.

Gee, look at the time. I'm keeping you from the game. I'd better be going. I look at him.

He's not moving. My English coach is smiling, warmly. I relax.

"You really like football, don't you?"

"Oh, yessir. It's the most wonderful game in the world. I used to love just defense. Knocking people down. Trying to guess where they were going, you know. Tackling people and everything. But now Coach has me playing offense, too, though I still get to play linebacker, of course. That's my favorite, you know, because you get a split second more reaction time and you're in on more tackles. But I'm getting to like offense too pretty much, although it's tricky, you know, with all the different plays and stuff and you have to do more set things. But that's okay really because learning the offense side helps me on defense. You know, to figure out what's happening, or going to happen. And the other way around, too, I suppose. Because I like defense best really. But I guess I said that."

The teacher nods. He's not even out of breath. "You're very expressive about football."

Expressive. Expressive? That's what Mrs. Guy said about me back in the fourth grade when I would dominate Show-and-Tell with endless tales and jokes that made everyone laugh and me feel good. I had had to look it up in the dictionary. It was good.

"Have you ever written about football?"

"No, sir. I just play it."

"Maybe you will write about football someday. The best writing comes when the writer is passionate about his subject."

I knew there was no way anyone could ever capture the feeling of football and confine it to a page of paper. Football is too fast to be written. It changes colors and shapes by the second. No two games, no two plays, no two moments even are ever the same. Each player's skill level and emotional chemistry are always changing between games, even within them, creating new opportunities and new weaknesses to mask. And you don't see many writers playing football. They might get their fingers bent and everyone knows writers need their fingers. Football doesn't have enough symbols for them or metaphors or something. The best symbol for football is an elbow. No, football has to be lived and savored quickly, like eating a bowl of potato chips, here this minute and gone the next. Too fast to savor. Writing takes too much time. You start analyzing a bowl of potato chips and they'll go stale before your eyes.

"Well, I like football, sir. But I'm not a writer."

"Not yet. But then you weren't always a football player either, were you?"

"Well. No."

"You probably didn't always like it."

Wait a minute. Was this English teacher in our living room, too, back in front of that tiny twelve-inch screen on that overcast Saturday afternoon?

"Uh, no, sir. I didn't always like it. You see, I didn't always know about it."

"You probably played baseball instead."

Now hold on here! This guy has been talking to my parents. But we hadn't had Parents Weekend yet.

"Yes. I liked baseball a lot. But I wasn't very good at it."

"But you tried it."

"Well, sure, sir. Everybody plays baseball." Ah-ha, that's how he knew about baseball.

"I thought," he continued, "football was pretty boring at first, watching it anyway. Then I played some and I very much enjoyed it. There's a lot to it, isn't there?"

I nod in awe.

"How'd *you* learn that you liked football?"

Cornered. All right, I give up.

"I tried it."

"Hmmm," he said. "You tried it and you liked it."

This guy sounded like Mom about some new yellow vegetable she had dug up.

He let the trying bit sink in a few seconds and mix with the writing idea.

So that's what he was up to. He wanted me to write a theme about football. People should only write about what they have to write about, choosing a topic from the teacher's list of approved ideas because then, you know, the necessary research books are on reserve in the library already. Writing was like eating beans, endless chewing for what? The taste of mud, that's what. It was fun to read. But not fun to write with all that thinking. Analyzing football or anything pleasant sucked all the fun and life from it. All that thinking about meaning and all that time spent sitting for what? A bunch of pale words on pieces of paper that couldn't even knock a fly down unless you rolled them up.

Still, I did need one more theme for this grading period. What harm could it do to write about football in a theme with a readership of one (three if you got an A, or a B+ with good comments, and sent it home)?

"People can express themselves in all kinds of ways," the English coach said.

Oh, yeah, well, besides painting, how? And poetry, yeah. Okay, and writing, too. Also, speaking. But besides that, how? Maybe dancing.

"The games they choose to play. Doesn't that say something about a person and his values?"

"I guess so, sir."

"And how they play those games."

"How they play them?"

"Sure. Do you always play football the same?"

"Yes, sir."

"So, if you have a fight with your roommate, you go out and play exactly the same that day as the day before?"

"Well, maybe I'd be a little angrier."

"Ah-ha. Anger is an expression of yourself, isn't it?"

I nod. This guy is like Mr. Wizard. I'm standing there looking at a blank wall and he walks right up and shows me a door that was there all the time. How'd he do that?

"And when you're losing badly, do you always play the same?"

"I try to, but it's hard. My father says—"

"And does everyone else on the team always try as hard?"

"No, sir. Some of them just fold up."

"And some of them play even harder, right?"

"Yes."

"Now, doesn't that tell you something about each one of them?"

"Yes, sir. It does."

"Like writing."

Ahh, how'd we get back here again?

"Or singing or playing the violin. Or doing lab research.

It doesn't just happen. It all takes hard work and creativity. And practice. And even the way you practice says something about you. Don't you think?"

"Yes, sir."

"Anything worth doing is worth doing right."

"My father says that. And the coach." And now you.

"Don't be afraid to try new things. If you'd been afraid to try, you'd never have tasted football."

That was great, tasting football. Perfect. I could not imagine a life without football. I was silent.

"No one can play football, or any sport, forever."

Who's talking forever? I'm living for next Saturday and, vaguely, the one after that.

"Maybe you should try writing someday?"

Maybe. Although there weren't any feet to watch and plays to dissect.

□ □ □

My senior year in high school football started with the usual boundless enthusiasm and unlimited promise. At eighteen, I was more familiar and comfortable with my body. It didn't seem to go off inexplicably and do things on its own so much while I had to watch. Feeling more in control, I was more confident, even outside my pads. I walked differently. I talked differently. I was in the best physical shape of my life, still short but pretty solid.

I had climbed above the clouds of considerable uncertainty. My grades had soared. I was trying a number of new activities—drama, the school newspaper, the yearbook, even the precision drill team. I had been designated a cadet officer. And although I obviously would never write a book, I was reading them with an eye to their construction. How on the surface, when you consumed them, they looked like one thing. But when you paused and took apart some sections, they were really carefully-constructed, intricate creatures with hidden wires and motivations secreted deep within. You'd start reading a part thinking it was headed in one direction and suddenly, through sarcasm or something, you realized the narrator had faked you out and you were headed down a different path to an idea that you'd never really thought about that way before.

Alone, the individual words were plain old familiar words on simple paper, like a playbook. But each author had his own style. He used the same words differently, buffing up a little-used side of a word or an image. And by arranging these familiar words into differing patterns with varying cadences and rhythms, these writers could convey a vivid picture with characters who lived and talked and performed just for me. And even though, of course, most of these writers were dead, their writing somehow lived on, as if a piece of them did, too. None of them described absolutely everything in a scene. And even though I had never been to any of the books' locales, I was able to fill in the blank spots accurately so that, I was certain, the scene in my mind looked exactly the way it had when it really happened in the writer's mind.

Each time I read a particular passage it came alive like the colored figures in the Sunday comics sitting there frozen on paper until someone picked them up. Then all the characters and action sprang to life. But each time I read a passage of a book, I read it differently, depending on my mood, my fatigue, my recent experiences and thoughts, the sounds around me. Each time I read I'd see another level or two of meanings. The same words were just printed on paper, but they were alive and changing, like a sunset or a floating cloud.

I was very much intrigued by detecting and deciphering these levels of handiwork. More precisely, I was fascinated by watching the author's footwork, by disassembling the author's prose machinery, by learning how he set a scene, how he created this mood, sketched this character, dropped this feint, crafted this impression, foreshadowed that doom. Not that I'd ever use them myself, of course, but I could appreciate the tools and the craftsmanship and enjoy the unlocking process like I had with Dad and Bobby Avila at those first games.

□ □ □

And then one afternoon disaster struck. It was the very beginning of the football practice season. Coach announced tryouts for quarterback, which seemed a little late but didn't concern me because I played fullback. Our first-string quarterback had graduated. There was no obvious heir-apparent, just a couple of seniors who'd played for several years and seemed destined to make our team's handoffs all season. No one had announced it; we just assumed it.

But then, out of the blue, the coach said he was going to have three guys try out to be his quarterback. That sounded like extra practices to me, which would be great, except for the wind sprints. He announced the names of the three candidates. One of them sounded like mine, but I had my helmet on and I didn't pay much attention because that was obviously ridiculous. I was a fullback, the fullback.

One trouble with things that seem so obvious in books is that they often aren't. Judging by the looks of a few players, they thought they had heard my name mentioned, too. So I wasn't stupid. I stood there with everyone else while two of the candidates went off to warm up with coach. The rest of us were apparently going to exercise over here. I started doing some stretches.

The coach stopped and looked back. So did the two quarterback candidates. "Mr. Malcolm?"

"Yes, sir!"

"Would you like to join us over here?"

"Uh, no. No, thank you, sir."

Everybody froze. What had I done? The coach walked back to me slowly. He had my utmost attention.

"Mr. Malcolm," he said. "That was not an invitation."

So why is there a problem then with me staying here?

This was baffling, like talking to my Grandmother Malcolm sometimes. Maybe coach wanted me to fill in until the missing third guy showed up. This was almost certainly going to be my last year playing football, so it would be a shame to waste even one hour of it in someone else's position. Maybe that third guy would be along real soon. Maybe—

Jesus H. Christ! I *was* the missing third guy! He wanted me to try out for quarterback. Quarterback! Team leader. Play caller. Official thinker. Strategy organizer. Field general. Squad disciplinarian. Signal caller. The only one to talk in the huddle. The only member of a football team who doesn't get to play football.

Linebackers are always trying to kill quarterbacks. Quarterbacks are always trying to fool linebackers or, worse yet, run away from them. Quarterbacks are always handing off the ball to someone else who gets to run into opponents. Quarterbacks are told to avoid injuries when running with the ball by falling to the ground just before the drooling linebacker arrives to deliver his destiny. Quarterbacks are always tossing the ball away just before they get tackled. Quarterbacks are quick.

Ahh, that's it. Coach probably forgot about me. I'll remind him that I'm not quick. He'll hit his forehead with the palm of his hand. "That's right, Malcolm. What was I ever thinking about? Thank you so very much for reminding me. I meant to say, Malone was the third quarterback candidate."

I'll forgive the coach for being fallible just this once. "That's okay, Coach," I'll say. I'll pat him on the back. And I'll turn and return, at a trot, to my rightful and satisfying place in the world as fullback and chief ball basher, hopefully handing out somewhat more punishment than I accept. Happy trails to me.

"Coach," I said as we walked quickly across the grass. "Coach. Coach, can I talk with you a minute?" Better be extra polite. "Please."

The coach halted. Politeness always pays. He turned toward me. He put both his hands on my shoulder pads. He looked me square in the face mask. And he paused. I recall smiling.

"No," he said.

Then he smiled and walked away. Without looking, he motioned with his arm to follow along.

By age eighteen I knew a few things about life. I knew playing quarterback was boring. I knew it was not for me. In fact, I knew I was not for it. I also knew to do what I was told. So I went along.

The trials lasted about a week. The three of us took turns calling the plays we were told to call, standing behind center, handing off the ball before we got tackled, passing the ball before we got hit, pretending to have the ball so we would get hit. The other two guys looked much more comfortable in the position. Not surprising, I guess, since they had played it before. My signals were clear. My handoffs were sharp. My fakes were pretty good. My passes stunk; they looked like tossed pillows, with both receiver and defender often stopping to await the ball's arrival. You don't throw footballs like shotputs.

I had briefly considered doing as poorly as possible to ensure that I lost the quarterback competition and returned to the spot that God intended me to play. This would have the added benefit, should I really lose the competition, of enabling me to say, semihonestly, that I didn't really want to win anyway.

But, I quickly realized, two things worked against me taking a fall. One, there was no guarantee I could have my old job back for the asking, especially if I had spent an entire week running around like a klutz and, perhaps transparently, making intentional mistakes. It made sense that I'd get my old job back, but it had also made sense that I never lose it in the first place.

Second, I knew my father would want a full report on the week's activities. As always, especially if I lost, that conversation would include the traditional question: "Well, did you do your best?"

I could reply "Sort of." But then he'd press me. I could never outright lie to him. I'd have to tell him the truth: "No." Oh, God, I could never do that. I couldn't stand the thunderous shame of the ensuing silence.

That meant I'd have to do my best, which wasn't that good anyway. But at least when I told him I lost the job that I didn't want, he'd say, "That's okay, so what did we learn from this?"

What I'd learned was that I couldn't pass worth shit and that you shouldn't go after jobs that other people want you to go for. I was sure Dad would then come up with a couple more pragmatic lessons.

So I did the best I could, which didn't turn out to be as hard as I thought because I really hate to lose and I knew more than I had thought about quarterbacking, just from watching those yahoos. The blond ones belong on surf-boards. I might take third place again, but, once more, it wouldn't be from choice.

I was not, let's be clear, lightning-footed. And I never could fall down and slide on purpose when tackle by some groaning neanderthal was imminent. Oh, you wanna play freight train, eh? Okay, well, I do this, too, on defense. SMASH. We'd run right into each other straight up, *mano a mano*, boy, I'll-show-you-stupid. It felt great. Nobody won. But more importantly, nobody backed down. I might be temporarily playing quarterback, but I could dish out some punishment, too.

Getting up, I'd sneak a peek over at coach, who'd be shaking his head again and looking down, no doubt, at some beetle in the grass.

Or if the guy came in low, I could give him some hip for a second, then whip it away and at least fall forward for another yard. Thank you, sucker.

The end of the tryout week came kind of quickly actually. It had been an interesting challenge, necessarily brief. But now it was time to get back to basics and get serious for the oncoming season. I was practicing looking a little disappointed while congratulating the winning quarterback. It would make him feel good, was cost-free to me, and maybe he'd give me the ball a little more in the regular games.

At the end of practice, coach called everybody to gather around him on one knee, which, next to being on your back on a wrestling mat, is one of the most uncomfortable positions of all time, wearing all those pads that aren't made for kneeling on one limb. But that pose does look real football and coaches, who don't wear thigh pads, aren't the ones who have to scrub the knees of football pants. (How many mothers, I wonder, have wanted to ask their sons, "How come the right knee is always dirtier than the left?") So, anyway, every coach calls in his players and says, "Okay, men, take a knee." Being so literal-minded, I'd kneel down for a minute. And then I'd stand up.

"It's been a good week of work. It's been difficult for all of us, I know, to get any real rhythm down with different quarterbacks. But I think it was a necessary exercise. I think it was a good one. We all learned from it as a team, which is why we're out here, for the team. Don't ever forget that.

"Now, after careful consideration, the other coaches and I have decided, at least for the start of this season, to have our number-one quarterback be Mr. Malcolm. Okay, men. Run it in. Have a good rest. See you out here tomorrow at ten sharp or we'll get in some extra running."

I was stunned. I felt both crushed and delighted. There went the familiar fullback for the foreseeable future. But here came something new. I hadn't realized how hard I'd been competing. It felt good to come out on top. But at the same time it was very uncomfortable. It's fun going new places but simultaneously scary to leave familiar ones. And it was hard for me to accept that kind of personal winning.

Everybody trotted off to the showers. I took off my helmet, a sign of respect before addressing the boss. He was talking with his assistants but motioned, wordlessly, to wait one minute. Then, the others strolled off after congratulating me. "We're counting on you," said the line coach. That's the problem, I thought.

"Coach, could we please talk for a minute?"

"Sure," he said. We were standing beneath a big tree that's still there.

"Sir," I said, clearing my throat needlessly. "I appreciate very much the honor of your picking me as quarterback. I really do, sir."

Now how could I break this news to him without making him look stupid?

"But sir, I'm not the best quarterback out there." He was listening to me. He really was. I'd better make sure. "I'm not the best quarterback out there, sir."

He looked at me for further explanation.

"I'm slower than the other guys."

Coach nodded.

"How fast do you have to run to run a quarterback sneak?" he asked.

"Yes, sir, but I can't pass worth, uh, beans."

He nodded even more.

"You may have noticed, son, that our offense is oriented around the run."

"Yes, sir, but I don't slide when you tell me to."

He tilted his head and nodded, yup, that's right.

"And . . . and I don't know the sequences for plays."

"You'll learn or you'll sit on the bench."

The bench? Wait. Wait.

"But sir." I was getting desperate. "I don't want to play quarterback."

He looked me right in the eyes and squinted his some. "I don't remember asking."

I knew then I had lost the argument. Actually, I never had a chance. Only in my young mind was there a hope that this man who had coached over three decades of pubescent punks would cave in to the power of my whining.

"Now, look," he said, and I was impressed by his confidential tone. "I'm not looking for a passer. I'm not looking for a professional. I'm looking for a young man to play high school quarterback. He doesn't have to be fast, but he does have to be a leader out there. You can be the best passer in Indiana, but if you can't get ten other boys to follow you into the fourth quarter down by ten points, then we'll have a royal case of chaos around here. And a record to match. And this'll be the longest autumn you ever knew. You wanna be a good fullback on a disastrous team?"

"No, sir."

"I think you're a leader. The other coaches think you're a leader. We need a leader. So you're our quarterback. It's best for the team. Let's see what you can do."

I must say I was wavering. He was treating me as if I was someone special. His showtime impatience of practice was gone. In its place was a respect and an exciting expectation. He almost had me convinced. There was only some slight steam left in my resistance. "I just want to play football, Coach. There's too much thinking at quarterback."

"Wait a minute," he said. "You give away sixty pounds to some of these guys and you still run into them. Are you afraid of failing, Andy?"

Of course I was.

"Of course not, Coach."

"All right," he said, acting a tad impatient. "It's called growing up, son. Get used to it. Now get in the showers, have a good rest, and be out here a half hour early tomorrow. I want to go over some technique with you. You've got a lot to learn in a short time. And I don't think you want to let your teammates down."

Thirty extra minutes of football? A private tutorial with the coach? You know, this leadership business just might have some potential after all.

□ □ □

I called my father that evening after study hall. "Hi, knucklehead. What's up?" he said.

"They picked me to be quarterback." He heard the distinct lack of enthusiasm.

"Congratulations," he said anyway.

"I don't know."

"You don't know what?"

"I don't know if I want to. Or if I can."

"They gave you a choice?"

"Well, no. He said I was the quarterback."

"Okay, there's no choice. That eliminates one question."

"I guess."

"What do you mean you don't know if you can?"

"Just what I said. I don't know if I can do a good enough job."

"Are you afraid of failing?"

What is this? Do dads and coaches go to the same school or something?

"Well, yeah, maybe. I don't know. I never—"

"That would be normal, you know."

"What would be normal?"

"To wonder if you can do the job."

"It is?"

"Sure. I wonder about every new job I take on."

"You do?"

"Sure."

"You never look like you're wondering."

There was a pause and I could hear him smiling on the phone.

"Quarterbacks aren't supposed to give away the play either, are they?"

"But I've never played quarterback."

"I imagine your coach knows that, don't you?"

"Yeah. Oh, sure. I told him."

"And judging by your team's record last year, having a whole lot of quarterbacking experience doesn't guarantee wins."

"No, I guess. But I'm a terrible passer and I'm not fast

and there's so much to running the offense. So much thinking."

"You call the signals on defense, don't you?"

"Sure."

"What's the difference?"

"Well, I—"

"And you do some thinking about defense, I hope."

"Sure, but that's defense."

"I'd think that your experience on defense would help
you on offense. And the experience on offense might make
you a better linebacker."

"You think? Really?"

"It sounds to me like your coach is looking for a leader."

"That's what he said. How'd you know?"

"We both manage personnel."

"Well, I'll do my best."

"I'm sure you will. If you didn't, you'd know it in your
heart. And you'd always wonder how good you really were.
Remember, you can always do whatever you have to do."

"Yeah. Yeah."

"Hey, knucklehead. Some people would trade an arm
and a leg to be in this position. If the coach thinks you can
do the job, what makes you think you know better than he
does, that you can't?"

"I don't know. It's a little scary."

"Good. Then you'll work a little harder."

□ □ □

Next day I was out on the field an hour early. So was the
coach. I got my warm-ups out of the way quickly. The
lessons began at the bottom—my stance behind the center,
scanning the entire field en route from the huddle, the
position of my hands to receive the ball, to move it, to hand
it off, and to seem to hand it off. He was big on efficiency
of motion ("You don't need all those tiny little steps. Just
pivot and hand off") and fakes. Coach loved fakes. We

practiced them endlessly: give it to one back, fake it to the next, pretend to keep it yourself and head around the end. Now fake it to the first back, give it to the second, pretend to keep it. Then fake it to the first two backs and really keep it myself. Now do the same thing to the other side. Time after time. "Stick that ball in there like you mean it. It's not a box of eggs; it's a football."

Coach would stand across from me like an opposing line-backer watching for telltale hints. "No, no," he'd say. "You're giving it away. When you're going to the right, you put your right foot back before the snap and when you're going left, you put your left back. Now, pick a stance and keep it every time."

We worked over and over on the fakes. "C'mon, Andy. Sell it to me. Sell. Sell. Look like you mean it. That's it. Keep me guessing. Don't make it easy. All you need is a moment's confusion."

In succeeding days he started making it more complex, adding hypothetical situations. "All right, second and one at midfield."

"Quarterback sneak?"

"Not bad. Or a 24- or 33-dive."

When the other coaches arrived, I'd be included in the strategy talks, mostly listening but they didn't shoo me away. This quarterback business was like a ladder up into adulthood. And every sentence overheard was a chance to learn something new and helpful. It was very exciting. I felt very grown-up.

The rest of the team was very patient with my newness, running through extra repetitions ordered by the coaches for my missteps. Some evenings after study hall the first-string offensive unit got together out on the lawn to run some plays in near-total darkness. My idea was that if we could run the plays in the dark without bumping into each other, it would help us all know instinctively what everyone was doing in the daylight competition. The first night or two we stumbled all over each other. But then we got better. The more we worked together, the smoother we got and the closer we grew.

The actual games became an eagerly awaited test of all we had been doing and dreaming, a measurement of life's progress without the need to wait a few decades. I couldn't wait each week.

On paper, the goal looked simple, even dull: Get the ball across the goal line and win some intangible points that had absolutely no worth outside the chalk confines of that field. Every game, even every scrimmage, began with that goal and a general plan on how to accomplish that against the predictable proclivities of this particular opponent. But as soon as the fresh new competition began with the excitement of twenty-two young men running at each other, the contest became a living organism, an unpredictable shifting series of attacks, confrontations, and feints matched by counterattacks, counterconfrontations, and counterfeints, sometimes even counterfeit counterfeints. The contents, the goal, and the success of these moves varied by the moment with the constantly shifting emotional, mental, and physical strengths and skills and the durability and fatigue of the ever-changing combination of players on the field at that time. The reluctant removal or imaginative insertion of one player could change the entire chemistry, as could the sudden perception or momentary inattentiveness of one man.

For spectators, this complex rendezvous could seem to be merely a simple, even brutal, physical combat. But for those within the game, the same struggle was really over an invisible prize, momentum, which could carry its temporary owners high into the sky, like the exhilarating upward arc of a child's ride on a swing. The joy of that soaring ride was also intensified by the inevitable imminence of the downward swing, which might be delayed a moment or two if only we could strain a little more, hope a little harder.

Not even every player on the field could be aware of all

the complexities in the living game. But he did sense the collective camaraderie of a larger athletic family unit, a protective and disparate array of skills and personalities forged by adversity and united by athletic ambitions and human hope. This enfolding unit had its own mores and humor, its running jokes and superstitions, its non-exclusive cliques, even a wise father figure whose moods colored life at that moment but who, like a conscientious parent, was always present on the sideline. Just seeing him standing there in a familiar posture or pacing in his peculiar way was calming. We didn't always want his dictums or advice, but we did always want to know that we could get them if we wanted them.

These football games created long periods of deliciously tense terror tinged with hope and marked by moments of exquisite ecstasy when everything, or enough things, clicked together. Also intense disappointment and frustration, which could be expunged by even more diligent preparation for the next week's contest.

I loved the combination of mental mind-games and physical body-games. Being on the football field, having practiced and strained and paid my dues, gave me a license to be the real me, better than I looked, smarter than many thought, tougher than some expected. Off the field, I had to rein myself in, to pretend I knew things I didn't, which often works in the nonathletic world. On the field, phonies got flattened. Off the field, in the real world, there was an endless amount of time to diddle and dally and blow hot air about ideas and plans. Society claimed to have a complex network of rules that everyone hailed, some obeyed, and even fewer enforced. Over the years more and more people came to notice that most of these much-touted sanctions were without muscle.

But on the field, the clock was always running, putting a high value on quick thinking, precise phrasing, and ingenuity. Players who produced hot air quickly had it knocked out of them. Infractions were usually spotted and always punished, right now, this minute, no matter who you knew or were. No appeals, no whining, no sixth chance to straighten up. Just shut up. Take the penalty like a man. Then suffer your teammates' condemning silence as the set number of yards were marched off against your side. Punishment was clean, efficient, just, certain.

There were always personal battles under way—sometimes, even wars—which the coach did not approve of but accepted as long as they did not detract from the team's effort. Meekness was not prized. There was a gruff, mutual respect; a decorum, an etiquette enforced by elbows and spikes and penalty flags.

Football provided a measurable and immediate achievement or failure on the field every single play. Eleven men on each side, dozens of plays in a game, broken into four precise quarters with progress or its absence measured in yards, and victory or defeat in points displayed in lights for all to see. Yeah, yeah; it would all help me later. I knew this because Dad had told me; "everything is practice for something," he said, which is the kind of thing adults said in those days.

"Yes, I know," I said, because already knowing everything seemed important in teen life. It still does to some. "Minus to a plus," Dad would say, implying the need to prepare for so much more of everything to come after today. But, frankly, I was thinking, "Screw later—the now is better."

Certainly the now was more intense. Playing football was a capsulized drama that rewarded those who could think ahead, quickly, while it erased the need to think of anything in life beyond this half.

"Take it easy," the coach was always saying during our hurried sideline conferences. "We've got plenty of time."

Plenty of time? Plenty of time? How could he be so damned calm with only six and a half minutes left and us down by six with the ball on our own forty-two, facing third and seven, when our longest run of the day had been five yards? He was infuriatingly calm. Didn't he know what was at stake here? I thought he'd coached so much. How could he miss the import of our predicament here?

But he put his hand on my shoulder pads, which I could feel anyway, and he looked out over the field, as if he was getting the play from somewhere else.

"All right," he said. "I want you to run a fake 34-dive, hold it a count to bring everybody up, and then I want you to hit Taylor over the middle eight yards down."

I looked at him in terror. A pass? You want me to pass the ball?

He answered my silence. "Yes, a pass."

"But we never pass."

"That's why it'll work."

From my vast football experience, I knew this was going to be a disaster. The coach had fallen badly in my esteem. How could he have forgotten everything he had seen in our passing practices, everything I had told him about my passing ability? But, of course, I could not argue.

"I'm not asking you to throw it the length of the field, son. Just a nice easy eight-yard toss to your end, who'll be waiting. Remind him to hold his block first for a second. And for God's sake, make sure you do a good job selling that fake dive. Take your time. Do it just like we did in practice."

Practice? There was nothing at stake in practice. This was a real live game with hungry linebackers and defensive linemen with no faces, just clawing hands. Let me outta here. If I'd still been fullback, I'd have been free of this planning hassle, waiting out there in the huddle to surely hear my number called, and then to plunge powerfully, carelessly, and mindlessly into the fray and try to battle ahead for twenty-two feet. Might would make right. It could be done. It could be done. And if I didn't make it the whole way, we'd have to punt, and I'd get to play linebacker some more. Some punishment for failure.

But now I was the leader. I had to carry in the coach's

message, which was completely different from what anyone expected. I had to sell it to my buddies, who would see right through my passing incompetence in a flash. They might even chuckle out loud and unsuccessfully seek to cover their smiles from me. And then in the face of eleven of the devil's disciples, I had to execute my first pressure-pass play, which only looks simple when it's on paper.

I turned to the coach and opened my mouth.

"Shut up!" he said. "Now just do what I told you. It's nothing we haven't practiced."

I nodded. I trotted back out, swearing silently. In the huddle, they looked up at me, expectantly.

"All right, guys. Fake 34-dive, right toss. Hold your blocks. George, don't forget to block a count and make sure you're past the marker before you cut. But look back right away in case I'm in trouble. All right. Listen carefully now. On two. Break!"

I took my time approaching the line. I surveyed the entire field. I only saw the middle. Wide open. Everyone was cheating up toward the line, certain that the fullback would get the call. I looked back at the backfield. I put my hands under center. Without thinking, I yelled, "Ready. Set." Our guys each put one hand down. It was our standard move, though I said it with an uncharacteristic sharp emphasis. The defensive tackle, too eager to become a hero, leaped offsides and slammed into our tackle.

The ref's whistle blew. The flag sailed. My smile emerged. Offsides. Five yards for the good guys. Fifteen feet less that my sodden pillow pass would have to travel.

In the huddle again. "Easiest five we've ever made, eh?" Half the guys smile. "All right, same thing. Hold those blocks, guys. On two. On two. Break!"

I surveyed again. They were crowded up again, even more certain of the line plunge this time. The ball slammed up into my hands. I whirled and obviously handed off to the fullback, who was so convinced that I was handing it to him that he went to hold on. I pulled it back, hid it against my hip, while I faded away from the action and the entire defense swarmed onto the fullback. One count, two counts. Casually, I looked back. And then, more seriously, beyond. There was my target loping across the field, unhindered, looking at me. Their safety had come up, but not all the way.

I lobbed the ball toward our end. He caught it. The surprised safety arrived a second later. The end carried him for another six yards. First down!

I was ready to celebrate. I looked over. The coach was checking his notes to call the next play. I see, we gotta get on with business. We did. We scored. Then I was really ready to celebrate. The coach was all business. "They've got three minutes to make something happen," he said, ominously. They tried. They passed. We won.

I thought surely the coach would want to drive home his dictum about hanging in there in those dark third and fourth quarters, no matter what. Hanging in there is a whole lot easier to say than to do, I find. Hopelessness, fueled by fatigue, can sprout so easily, like dandelions that pop up and flourish in any available spot.

But no. The coach and I shook hands. He gave me a smile and a few words. "I guess you can do it," he said. Which made me feel good, no matter that Dad had been saying the same thing for years. This was The Coach speaking. At the team meeting I virtually repeated his words: "See," I said, "we can do it." And I think from that third down play, we all started to believe.

□ □ □

Winning tastes good. And the harder we had worked, the sweeter it tasted. Winning got to be a most pleasant habit. The weeks and the games took on a comforting rhythm, except for the ubiquitous windsprints. Mondays, which had yet to take on that tired here-we-go-again aura of adulthood, were low-key reviews of the past game and the initial introduction to the next opponent. Tuesdays and Wednesdays had lots of drills on basic skills, maybe two or three new plays geared for a particular opponent, and forty-five minutes of scrimmaging to keep the intensity up. Thursdays had no full-speed hitting and Fridays had conditioning and light walk-throughs of plays without full pads.

The coach had been on me all the time about unnecessarily running into people as the quarterback. "But Coach," I said, "I run into people all the time on defense and you don't mind."

"That's your job on defense," he said. "On offense there are smarter ways of beating people."

Maybe smarter, I thought, but not as much fun. First, he took away my fullback job and all its sporting spontaneity. Then he made me do all this thinking, which was getting to be more fun, actually. But now he wanted me to give up my head-on intimidating collisions. I could always get away with it now and then, of course, by saying I thought I could pick up another yard or two. And if I did most of the time, coach would be hard-pressed to come down too hard, although my excuse was transparently self-serving.

However, I was intrigued by his next line: "Wouldn't it be frustrating to you as a linebacker if every time you went to level somebody who'd already gained several yards, he disappeared on to the ground so you couldn't?"

I thought that might be seen as chicken.

"Saying it's 'chicken' doesn't make it so," coach suggested, "if you've got a larger plan in mind."

Ah-ha, a sneak plan! What is it?

"Keeping you healthy to run the offense."

Yes. And?

"And that's it. If you run into him just to show him how tough you are, and you get hurt and can't run the offense, who's won that battle?"

Maybe it'd be the linebacker who'd get hurt, not me.

"A linebacker can play with a broken hand. You can't."

What is it with adults that they always know so much

147

and the obvious lesson always has to do with having less
fun?

"So you have your fun running into people when you
don't have to and your teammates pay the price. That's not
leadership, Malcolm. And it's not smart."

Damn. He'd trotted out the Selfish Stratagem. There's
no defense against that on a team sport. I started sliding,
although I didn't stop giving myself the ball on offense.

Guess what coach said. That was okay as part of a strategy. "But a big part of leadership is not trying to do everything yourself. You play to other people's strengths and
convince them they can do it."

"Why should I waste all that time convincing somebody
they can do a job when I can just keep the ball and do it
myself? And that doesn't risk a handoff."

"How hard do you think he's going to block for you every
single play if he doesn't feel like a part of the team?"

Shit!

So I started giving the other guys individual pep talks.
And, pretty soon, everybody was feeling like an important
cog in an invincible machine. If Andy couldn't do something, Pat could or George or Bill. It was a very delicate
spiderweb of intersecting skills and relationships whose
strength under adversity was untested. But we were be-
lievers.

Sometimes, believing seemed like enough. Sometimes,
it was. Sometimes it wasn't. We had won three straight
games. Not just won them, dominated them. We were in
control virtually every minute. We didn't know how rare
that feeling would be in real life. But it was a very good
feeling on the field—and off it for a good number of hours
afterward.

And then came a nondescript opponent looking for a
moment of glory and sparking a close call. By all rights,
they shouldn't have had a chance. In real life, they wouldn't
have a prayer. In real life—say, a battle—they would have

marched into combat, hoping everything would turn out and, as underdogs do, hoping that hope was enough. They would, of course, be annihilated in a messy reality that every survivor would want to forget. And someday some Hollywood producer with a swimming pool and a driver would turn this sad tale into a modern entertainment about how courageously some pathetic souls marched to their certain extinction.

But this was a football game where hopes, like adrenaline, can fuel heroic fantasies and surprising outcomes. We played evenly for most of the game. With a quarter of a quarter left, it was a scoreless tie, which was an inspiring victory for them and an ominous cloud for us.

We had the ball just inside our own territory. Things that had always worked before didn't that day for no reason that I could discern; such reasons only become clear when you see the movie of the event. So it seemed like a good idea to try something new. How about a pass for a change? I don't know whose idea that was, probably mine copying the coach's ploy from the previous game. Maybe the other team's scout had remembered to tell his defense, which remembered at the right time. Maybe our line was tired or discouraged or just inattentive for one play. Maybe the other team was hungrier at the right time for them and the wrong time for us? I'll have to wait for the movie to learn what really happened.

Anyway, I faked the run again. I dropped back to pass. The protection of my line was crumbling. So was my self-confidence. I had very little time to think of alternatives. I had, in actual fact, no real alternatives in my repertoire. Our end was just making his cut, turning across the middle. They were in my face now, grunting, clawing. I saw George's face for an instant. Then I lost it. I threw the ball to where I thought he would be two instants from now.

He wasn't.

They were.

A defensive back intercepted the pass. Throwing that

ball was a dumb, panicked thing to do. Simply falling down and taking a short defeat on that play but keeping the ball in order to punt it and maybe steal it back did not occur to me. I was not yet wise to the reality of hope. There was no time for reorganizing or consoling. They had seized the momentum. Piece by piece, with no tricks, just admirable determination, they marched in halting spurts down the field. They scored: 6–0. Joy for them. Despair for us.

We blocked their extra point try. Joy for us. Despair for them.

The score remained 6–0.

We lined up for the kickoff. It was a formality. Less than a minute left. None of us had played sharply that day. But I had won the game for the enemy. They had not beaten us. I had lost it. I grew strangely quiet, the kind of sullen silent that parents choose not to disturb for a couple of hours. No one came near me, not even the coach. I knew what was about to happen now. They'd intentionally kick the ball on the ground. It would bounce all over unpredictably, consuming seconds. One of our linemen would pick it up, possibly start to run the wrong way, desperately look for someone to lateral to, and end up being tackled where he stood. We'd use up our remaining timeout trying to stall the clock. One or two of my desperation dead-duck passes would fall short. We'd lose.

Unless in their excitement the prematurely ecstatic enemy made a mistake.

They did.

Maybe their kicker forgot the basic strategy for a kickoff with only seconds remaining. Maybe they'd forgotten to practice onside kicks this week. Maybe the kicker was rattled by the extra-point try when his kick had been slapped back into his face. Maybe he was just dumb.

His kickoff sailed high and deep into our territory. Oh, my God! We would have a chance to run it back! Fast and far. Oh, my God, there was hope in hope. Oh, my God, the ball was coming toward me, drifting end over end down and down. Oh, my God, redemption was at hand. Oh, my God!

I looked that ball into my arms. I tucked it away so firmly not even Dad could strip it. My eyes quickly scanned the field. In the huddle, a very calm coach had assumed they'd try a short onside kick, which would eliminate the risk of a long return and force some risky improvisation, which was the point of squibbing kicks like that. But just in case (there were a lot of "just in cases" on our coach's team), he called for any kickoff return to come down the right side. My blockers up front were already moving to our right. So, reading our players, were the defenders.

I went to the left.

There was a stunned pause. Suddenly, the undisciplined defenders, who could see me, started washing back to the other side to head me off. Each of them had an assigned lane to cover to prohibit any lengthy runbacks. It's that basic football lesson—"Stay in your lanes," the coaches always yell. But our opponent's excitement, the team's inexperience, and my seeming misdirection had turned the forced improvisation table around on them. The distinct lanes were becoming fogged. A seam might open up for me to squeak through. Then again, it might not.

My blockers, unable to see me, continued to set up a return lane down the right sideline. At about the thirty-five-yard line, I veered right again behind the protective wing of blockers, who thought I'd been there all along. The earnest eagerness of the defenders had caused many of them to run themselves right out of the play.

One would-be tackler got through. I ran him over. Nothing was going to stop me this time, not even my onetime eagerness to run into opponents needlessly. My mind had clicked into gear to handle this situation. From despair I had shot up to determination, all in seconds. It felt good to have the initiative. I don't remember ever running faster in my entire life. I wasn't thinking about scoring a touchdown. I was thinking about my next step, and the next one, and the one after that. Feet reaching, knees up, ball in my outside arm; if I lost control of it, the ball would fall out of bounds and remain in our possession. If I got cornered, I could step out, too, and stop the clock.

I was near the sideline now. I ran in silence, looking left. But I could sense the stands and my teammates on the sideline jumping up and down soundlessly in my sweaty vision. The crowd of players was behind me now. There was but one defender to destroy. I veered slightly toward him, then ducked away without touching. He was bracing for an impact that did not come and found himself clutching air. I was gone. The last forty yards were wide open. But I poured it on anyway as fast as my short, thick legs would go. In the end zone I gently set the ball down; act like you've been there before, boys.

Moments later, I was surrounded by ecstatic teammates and fans. With defeat in sight, we had tied the game. And I had been the ballcarrier. An eighty-six-yard endeavor when everything had seemed hopeless. Then, through grit and not giving up, we surged back in the nick of time. Perseverance paid. All we had to do now was kick the thing through the goalposts and carry off a miraculous comeback, 7–6. My God, it was a happy moment! We had done it! I had done it! What would the coach say? He might even smile. Wait'll I phone Dad! How sweet this was! I couldn't wait to hear him smile. We turned a minus into a plus, big-time.

They were picking me up now. The cheers were resounding. My smile was immense. The celebration was deliciously spontaneous. And then, slowly, regretfully, painfully, as if the joyous crowd had suddenly grown up in one instant, they were setting me down. The cheers died. The referee was waving us back. A flag on the play. One of our linemen, in his own eager earnestness, had blocked a defender in the back. I hadn't seen the illegal block; it had happened way behind me out of the action. An irrelevant infraction in the heat of battle that negated everything. Fifteen yards penalty from the spot of the foul. We got the ball just slightly ahead of where I had caught it. My herodom vanished.

Now, on the other side, the despair evaporated. The ecstasy emerged. Twenty-five seconds to go. Could we pull off a second miracle in a minute?

Nope.

Two dead-duck passes fell worthlessly to the ground. I had just presided over a new invention; we had managed to lose the same game twice. I was speechless with hidden pain. The other team was unable to speak either, but their incoherent yells and whoops were sufficient.

A heavy door slammed shut on my emotions. I had none. I was not going to give anyone any satisfaction in this bitter defeat. This loss was my fault. My steel-face was in place. We got in line to shake hands. "Good game!" many of them said. I did not reply.

Their ebullient coach took my arm. "I told him," he said, not needing to identify the kicker, "whatever you do, don't kick it to you! So what does he do? Nice try, son! Nice try!"

I hate those words. I hate those words more than I can write, even now, over three decades later. What's nice about a try that fails? I hated that coach as he ran off to celebrate their lone win of the year. I hated his players. I hated myself. I hated nearly everyone except, strangely, the lineman who had ruined our comeback. Chuck had been trying too hard, as I usually did. He'd be suffering in loneliness right now. Protocol forbid anyone chastising him, even the coach, although leaving him alone was not exactly endorsement of his action. Later, Chuck would apologize. "Sorry about that," he'd say, looking down at the ground.

"Hey," I replied, punching his fatty shoulder. "Forget it. I threw the interception that really lost it." Chuck would shuffle off and we would avoid looking at each other for many days, the sight of each of us being too painful a reminder.

No, except for Chuck, I was hating pretty much the entire world at that moment, even people I had never met in foreign countries where soccer was called football. Only three things can happen when you pass the football, I had now proven, and two of them are bad. If only I'd eaten the ball instead of giving it away, just fallen down, written off that play as a loss and lived to try another play. We could have had a scoreless tie, which, I imagine, is like kissing a sister. But right then, a scoreless tie seemed much better than a narrow loss that turned into a miraculous victory that turned into a bitter defeat.

I was walking off the field within a silent throng, each of us losers languishing in a vivid solitude. And then, I felt this vise close on my right arm above the elbow. It was extremely strong, which may be why I did not instinctively yank my arm away and turn to punch whatever was there.

I turned my head. It was an old man. No, it was the coach. "Stop!" he said.

I did.

I looked down at the ground. He put his hand under my face mask and forced my head up. He didn't have much to say. There wasn't much to say.

"One play either way does not make a football game," he said. "We had plenty of other chances to score and make that interception irrelevant. We didn't do it today."

I went to argue and shoulder more blame.

"Shut up!"

"Handling victory is easy, Mr. Malcolm. I want to see what you do with defeat."

He punctuated that sentence by poking his forefinger into my chest. Then he stared at me for a long moment.

What a dumb sonofabitch he was! What a stupid thing to say. Who needs to practice defeat? It finds everyone easily enough. Coach wanted to see me practice losing, as if we should all get ready to handle defeat after defeat throughout our lives. Well, we practice 34-dives and 48-pitches. Might as well practice 6–0 losses. Get us ready so we won't invest quite so much effort the next time, then we won't be quite so disappointed. Coach was the loser. Let him practice handling defeat. He was the coach who knew everything.

After all his talk about hanging in there, no matter what the score, no matter how much time was left, now my coach was reduced to watching to see whether his amateur quarterback had practiced losing well enough.

I was speechless. My mouth may have been hanging open. But he obviously packed a great deal of meaning and feeling into those words because his fingers left bruises on my arm. I stormed away. Alone is safer.

In the dorm, I went into the sacred solitude of the small shower. I locked the door. I stood under the water to wash away the anger, too. It didn't work. Why couldn't I be a more alert player? I knew you never threw anywhere you couldn't see. How could I be so weak? How could I forget a basic like that? Damn! I slammed the tiled wall with my open hand. Then with the side of my fist. Again. And again. Sonofabitch!

There was so much emotion to come out that I exploded into tears. Not sad, feel-sorry-for-yourself sobbing but straight-out, face-up, teeth-gritting tears full of rage. As soon as they emerged, the powerful stream of water washed them away. A half hour later, the storm had passed. I was not angry at anyone else, just me. And I was going to learn, once and for all, to obey my own merciless discipline. I would show me never to allow mental slips.

I was pretty silent that week, not sullen, chip-on-my-shoulder silent but intense, get-out-of-my-way silent. Practices were more businesslike than usual. I ran extra laps. When the coach told us to do forty push-ups, I did fifty. I did not have time for the usual jokes. I suggested somewhat more passing practice than usual. I called a few extra team practices after dinner. I talked a lot about focus. The guys did not grumble or resist any of this. They seemed to step up their own intensity level as the week went on.

On Wednesday I had a private meeting with myself. I wrote down a list of my transgressions from the previous game. I wrote down scribbled vows to prevent repetitions: "I will never pass blindly again." Fifty times I wrote the solution for each problem.

Then I set myself an outrageous goal for Saturday. I was going to score two, no, three touchdowns. I had never scored more than one in a game. Three was impossible. If I didn't get three, then the next week the punishment would be that I'd have to score four. Until I learned my lesson. I wrote this down two hundred times: "I will score three touchdowns. I will score three touchdowns."

It was selfish, of course. There are always personal goals and ambitions on teams, but there is no room for acknowledging them on a successful team. So I didn't tell anyone about the vows. At night, in bed, before falling asleep, I planned some touchdown drives, assembling plays that showed a pattern of proclivities and then produced an unexpected twist. I memorized the drives. If I was going to have to think while playing football, I was going to get my thinking out of the way beforehand. Clear the decks for the actual action of the game. And the fun. But the only fun that emerged that week was the fun of knowing exactly what we were going to do.

The intensity continued through the coin toss and the handshake. I nearly crunched the opposing captain's hand. Good luck to you, my ass. Prepare to be annihilated, sucker.

We always started our games with handoffs and dives up the middle for a few plays. It was safer until everyone shook off their pregame butterflies by getting in a few hits. The first play I called a fake dive. The defense knew our tendencies. They were ready for the dive up the middle. They swarmed all over the fake. I pitched to a halfback arcing around right end. Fifteen yards. The next play we did the same thing. Ten more yards. And again. Seven more. We'll be taking these yards as long as you're giving them, thank you.

They called time out. A time out in the first two minutes meant they were in disarray. It also meant they'd be ready for the pitch this time. We ran up the middle. Seven yards.

I didn't need to confer with coach. We marched right down the field, gaining yards on every play until it was first and ten on their eight. Power dive to the right. Second down on the four. Another dive to the right. Third down on the two.

Then we did a fake power dive right. I seemed to hand the ball to the first back through. He slammed in between guard and center. No, now I seemed to hand the ball to the second man through. He slammed in between guard and tackle. I stood up to see how well they had done. There was a big pile-up. But I had the ball on my right hip. I trotted away from the pile in a U-turn and squirted around the left end. Their defenders couldn't understand why our sidelines were cheering until they saw me alone in the end zone handing the ball to the ref.

We kicked the extra point.

On the way to line up for the kickoff I ran up to the coach. It made no sense to anyone but me.

"That's one," I said.

Coach did not reply.

We kicked off. They got two yards on the runback. On the first play, they lost three yards. We were coldly efficient, confident, eternally patient, silently oblivious to our opponent's suffering but knowing it was coming and, better yet, knowing that meant our inevitable victory. We were very patient that first quarter. For once. Patient and persistent. There was no hurry. We knew what we were going to do. We knew how to do it. We were determined to do it. We had no doubts about the outcome. Nothing personal. And they knew it, too. There was no mouthing off to each other. No celebrating, no yahoo yelling about being unstoppable. Just fairly precise execution. We'd grind out another four yards, get up, and return to the huddle, ready to do it again, and again. We'd smash their ballcarrier for a loss, get up, and line up for the next play, ready to go, before they had recovered from the disappointment of the last one. We'd been there before. Now we knew what to do—crush their confidence as well as gain our yards.

Each man performed his own assignment and was often alert to the little extras. When our first defender got to a ballcarrier, he went for the tackle. The second defender to arrive went for the ball. Strip it! When it looked like they were about to break something, down the far sideline perhaps, one of us would come streaking in from the other side and crush it. Not that person's job. But he'd been alert, ready to hustle over, to step in if needed. He was. So he did. It was a good example for all of us. Everything just flowed, as smoothly as unpredictable human games go.

We ran lots of dives up the middle in the first and second quarters to tire out their line for the third and fourth quarters. It wasn't our style to pass much. They knew that. It didn't matter. Four yards per play will keep possession of the ball, boys. And keep it away from them.

They didn't seem able to decide what to do. They tried all kinds of plays, seeking that elusive athletic chemistry of success, something, anything, that worked. But we weren't desperate. We were ready. Last week was history. Our huddle was silent, eyes on me. Tell us what coach says to do, Andy. So I did. And they performed. It felt good. Very good.

By the third quarter they were getting up slower. We'd bounce back up in fine shape, ready to resume play, right away. C'mon, let's go. This is fun. Once or twice, their trainer had to come out and coax a player up to limp to the sideline. Didn't matter to us. Who's next?

We scored again on a fullback dive to the right that turned out to pick up nearly fifteen yards. 14–0.

We stole the ball back and ground it down to the one-yard line. I didn't look over to coach for guidance. I'd gone over this scenario in my mind on Wednesday and Thursday nights. I called a quarterback sneak. I made it by a foot.

That's two.

I had to give them credit. They weren't giving up. But they weren't going anywhere either. Fourth quarter. Comfortably ahead, 21–0. We were at our own forty. They took Barry down for a loss of two yards. "Damn!" I said ostentatiously as we returned to our huddle. Third down and eight. We were in control of the game. I had a twist of an idea from the eighth grade.

"Punt formation," I said.

"Andy," said Pat gently, "it's only third down."

I nodded. I knew that. But were they—tired, dispirited—paying attention to the down? We'd soon see. If my idea didn't work, we'd still have fourth down to really punt.

"Fake punt, pass left. Make it look good. Hold the blocks, guys."

We lined up to punt the ball away, one of the few times that day. They were pleased with their minor triumph. Their safety, embarrassed because he had forgotten it was time to punt, hurried back to receive the kick. Their line prepared to charge. Maybe they could block the kick dramatically and ignite the emotions that launch an exciting and glorious comeback. It has happened.

No one was yelling from our sidelines about the apparent waste of a down. I knew coach knew something was up, he always watched so closely. "Always take enough time to use your head out there," he'd say.

No one was yelling from their sidelines—yet. Either they hadn't noticed. Or they feared alerting us to our own mistake. Then their coach realized. He started to race down the sideline, yelling. Too late, buddy.

Standing protectively between our line and our kicker, I quickly called the signals. The ball came floating back past me. Everybody managed to hold their blocks, except our left end. He was one of our best blockers, but their defensive end got by and came charging in. I went to stop him.

He might block the kick. What a disaster! But I, too, missed my block. Oh, no!

He thundered toward the kicker, eagerly, leaving me in his dust. I ran away, toward our left end. Then, I turned. There, barely four feet from my face was the ball, having drifted gently over the head of the surprised defensive end, who was turning his head to discover that anticipated moment of glory detonating behind his back.

I quickly adjusted my path so the ball would sail in over my left shoulder. I could get hit, any second now, blindsided by some lumbering line leviathan whose slowness happened to place him in position to destroy my moment of glory and seize it for himself. But our line had been methodical about holding their blocks until we seemed to get the kick away.

Can't worry about being nailed now. I watch the ball into my outstretched arms and hands, willing it to nestle in the proper place and, unconsciously, adjusting my hands to ensure that it did. "Make a basket," Dad would say. "Little fingers and elbows together. Little fingers and elbows. Look it in." The ball settled into place. Amazing how light and dainty some parts of a football game are. I tucked it under my left arm and headed downfield as quickly as my stubby legs would go. Everyone was behind me now, everyone except the startled safety. One moment he's preparing to run back a kick and uplift his team. The next he realizes they've been totally suckered and he's the one obstacle between his team and a mortifying disaster. He's likely embarrassed; I hope he dwells on that a few seconds, a helpful distraction. He's probably pretty pissed. He's certainly fast.

Instinctively, I consider turning into him. Let's go here, chump. You and me before every spectator and God and, oh, God, my coach. On second thought, I'd better angle for the sideline. He will, too. Try to ruin his angle of attack, to open the door a little wider for me than for him. It might work. It might not. But I've got the first down anyway no matter what.

I push myself. I'm puffing. I'm striding. I'm angling. He's flying over. I see the crowd on his sideline jumping up and down. He's calculated his angle on my initial speed. If I can find just a hair more, it'll ruin his plans. He won't have a tackling angle on me; he'll have to try and grab me with an arm as I zip through the intersection and he can't make the corner. Unless he just stretches and takes out my legs with his body like toppling a couple of bowling pins. That's what he should do, forget his arms, use his body. I've got no maneuvering room.

He's closer. I'm driving, standing upright, right arm pumping. He's going to have to earn this one. So am I.

Out of my right eye I see his right arm go up. I wait an instant, then I duck my shoulders down and twist them. His hand glances across the back of my shoulder pads. He flies on out of bounds, like an errant rocket. I'm home free now. Twenty more yards. Or am I? No time to look for other pursuers. I change my angle to the end zone to throw off any more approaching missiles. I pour it on, as much as I can anyway.

Sixty feet later I'm safe. I run out of the end zone just to make sure I've crossed every possible line. The points are earned. The vow is fulfilled. The victory is assured. The enemy is vanquished. The plans worked. The determination was delicious. The satisfaction was exquisite, made more intense by its precariousness at times. The whole thing tastes very good.

I trot up to the coach, amid our sideline glee. "That's three," I said.

He shakes my hand heartily. Then, he holds on to it, keeping me there. He looks me in the eye again. Now, here comes the warning about some mistake.

"Handling victory is easy, Mr. Malcolm. I want to see what you do with defeat." He smiles at me then, across the years that he saw awaiting me. Oh, I get it! I smile back.

□ □ □

There were other games that last fall of my brief football career. We won them all, save one, a 6–7 loss in the second game of the playoffs. Afterward, I hung around the locker room for a couple of hours, still wearing my sweat-soaked pads over the T-shirt that clung to my skin, the once-white socks caked with mud above the shoeline and still pristine beneath it, and the eyeblack that had run down my cheeks like male mascara. I knew it was the last time my whole being would tingle with the anticipation that comes when I sense the play was coming my way. I knew in my heart it was my last time in a locker room with my brothers. I knew it was the last time I'd lift off the confining helmet that matted my hair in wet clumps that felt so suddenly cool on my scalp, the last time I'd awkwardly pull off that brightly colored jersey, unlace the sodden pads and pants, and strip off the long socks that always turned inside out. I knew it was my last football game. I didn't want it to end. I hadn't wanted to let go of playing fullback. I didn't want to let go of the game. It had made my short life so rich and vivid.

"Memories are not such bad things to have," my father had told me once before when I lost something I loved very much. Well, I didn't want pale memories, a mental scrap-book I could trot out late on dark nights in bed when my mind inadvertently wandered to the most amazing places while I smiled until sleep came and everything got forgotten. I wanted the real thing. I knew I was nowhere near good enough for the semipro ball that was played at the Big Ten university I would attend. I knew that my link to football, like childhood, was sadly over for good. I knew nothing in life could ever be as good as actually playing football.

Little did I know.

□ □ □

The first toy I bought my first son was a four-inch plastic football. I washed it with soap under hot water and stuck it in his crib, in the corner where he could see it at any waking moment. Chris tried to nurse on it.

I bought a toy football helmet and some model airplane paints. I colored the helmet for the Cleveland Browns, which is not too difficult because it's the only team without a big letter or cartoon character in the logo. I put the helmet by his crib. Later, he would toddle around the living room with the oversized plastic hat wobbling all over his head. And my laughter and applause made him do it more.

When he began talking, we'd watch some games on television. "Here," I'd say, "watch this guy. He's called a guard. Look! Look, see what he did?"

From the start Chris preferred the high kicks and the long passes with their dramatic, excruciating waits that allow everyone to imagine all the delightful and disastrous consequences that are about to happen. "Oh!" he'd say. "Kick a ball! Kick a ball!"

Then when the kick returner was buried by defenders, "Oh, too bad."

No, I'd say, that's good. We don't want that man to get away. But Chris was into the offense from the beginning. He didn't want to defend against anybody. He wanted me to throw him the ball, time after time, weekend after weekend, so he could run away with it, if he managed to hang on. "No, here, like this, Chris. Put your little fingers and elbows together. Make a basket. Look the ball into it." Slow motion, holding on to the ball, I'd guide its flight toward and into his outstretched arms. Then, suddenly, we'd resume full-speed life and he'd run away, any way he could to dodge me, zigzagging to paydirt.

Gradually, we moved up to a full-sized ball, which took both of his arms to cradle, if he also used his chin. I was delighted. He seemed to enjoy it, too. Indoors or out, football brought us together, eagerly, at any season. He played street hockey and baseball, too, of course. And I tried to coach with the few insights I had. One particularly important baseball lesson involved not putting your fingers around the front of the bat when attempting a bunt.

We also followed the Browns games, the player draft, the player moves. Who was moving was irrelevant. The important point was that we learned about it and kept track of it for a day or so and each had our own immaterial opinion about it, which we could discuss after dinner or during our games of catch, which grew more elaborate as he and his physical skills grew.

I would create hypothetical game scenarios. I was the quarterback. He was the end. "Okay, Chris, we're six points down. Two minutes left. It's third and nine at mid-field." It was better than just standing there lobbing the ball back and forth with nothing at stake, and my theory was that if he ever did play football, if he ever did anything competitive really, pressure situations would at least be familiar. Another of those little pieces of straw that a parent picks up over all the years and unconsciously seeks to weave into something meaningful with no expectation of ever seeing results.

I'd give Chris a pass pattern to run. I'd call the signals. He'd run it. I'd lob the ball. He'd catch it. We'd celebrate. Now we had earned a fresh slate. One of us would provide a running play-by-play. It was first and ten. Do it again. Go for the long bomb. Can he do it? Yes? Oh, no, well, that's okay. My fault. I threw it too far.

But now it was second and ten. A little more at stake. "Ten yards is that crack in the curb. Don't catch any shorter than there. Okay? You've always gotta know where you are." Signals. He'd run. He'd cut. I'd throw. He might catch it. "Hurry back to the huddle. The clock is running. The clock is running." If he dropped it, the clock stopped. But now it was third and ten. We were running out of chances. "Oh, no, he dropped it. Fourth and ten. Can he do it? The pressure is on, folks. A minute and a half left, down by six points with thirty-five yards to go. But the young end looks calm and collected. Malcolm barks the signals. Malcolm runs down the street. Malcolm cuts to the left. The ball is in the air. And . . . he . . . dropped the ball. Oh, no. But wait. Wait! There's a flag on the play. Defensive holding. The good guys have one more chance. The clock is running, the clock is running.''

It was truly amazing how many penalties there could be on the defense. Every time Chris dropped the ball on fourth down, there was a penalty and he'd get another chance. "C'mon, Dad," he'd say.

"No, really, Chris. I saw him do it. But now the pressure is really on." We even bought a couple of white handkerchiefs and dyed them sort of yellow in a kitchen pot that never did come clean after that. But at least we had our own penalty flags to throw.

Sure enough, eventually Chris would catch the fourth fourth-down pass. And we would celebrate and gear up for the next set of downs, which had to be run without a huddle this time because, by now, the clock was way down and we had to score or we'd lose. And nobody could know the outcome because it was unfolding, live, before our eyes right then. Which was very exciting. Sometimes we even drew a retired neighbor or two as unpaying spectators who would reward a particularly stunning catch of Chris's with light applause.

Pretty soon, Chris was catching the ball pretty regularly. My favorites were the game-deciding catches made while falling out of bounds in the end zone. Or crucial first downs along the sideline. I'd wait until the last second to throw them. And I'd intentionally throw them just beyond his reach. Chris would run up to the curb, halt, look back, and reach out, way out, while keeping his toes hanging on the cement edge of the street. He'd stretch out so far. And if he could touch the ball with his fingertips, he'd always pull it in—before falling flat on the ground. "First down! Yes, ladies and gentlemen, the young end has done it again.''

I got such a kick out of seeing him make those sideline catches. If he ever did play real football later, he might want to try out for end. He wasn't tall or fast (now wherever did he get that from?), but he had very good eye-hand coordination. And he had also learned to hang on to the ball. "Strip it!" I'd yell suddenly from out of nowhere. I'd flail at the ball in his hands. And he'd hang on tightly. He would not fumble it. He would give me one of those cocky kid smiles silently saying, "See, Dad. I know you now."

At ten, Chris joined his first neighborhood youth league football team. We didn't live in that neighborhood, but they didn't have an abundance of players, especially an abundance of players who would show up for every practice as well as the Saturday morning games. There was no choice about practicing in my book. Practice was the player's ticket to play. "There's a lot more practice in life than there are games," I'd say without knowing exactly where that insight came from. But it sounded very fatherly.

The Saturday games were near-chaotic affairs at times. There were uniform shirts, but everything else was provided by each player, which produced a colorful array of helmets bobbing about on the undersized field. Not having shown up for many of the Tuesday and Thursday practices, not many of the players knew what to do. Some of the linemen thought they should be given turns to run the ball to glory. I remember the other end on Chris's team often lining up with his hands safely tucked in his pockets and then watching the play unfold like a spectator. But while the teaching of football fundamentals was informal at best, the coaching of the kids to keep trying and to channel their ambitions and energies according to the adults suggested rules was consistent. They had a good time running around bumping into each other, falling down, and being eagerly watched and applauded by their parents, who proferred much patting and encouragement anytime any player approached the sidelines.

166 ANDREW H. MALCOLM

The following summer Chris was recruited by a team in a distant neighborhood. This was a more serious team in a more serious citywide league. They had daily practices, a longer schedule, an intense coach, and games against similar-sized youngsters in a league that sprawled throughout the region. They also had impressive formal uniforms and, if earned, a championship game in the city's main stadium come November. Another major attraction was being recruited by the coach, a heady experience for young athletes (old ones, too).

I stressed to Chris the importance of his basic decision to join the team and the time, both travel and practice, this would entail. Once made in August, I did not regard his decision as a rescindable commitment. He chose to try. And every morning next to his school lunch money was his bus fare for the trip to practice. He'd do homework in the back of the bus, his feet resting on the pile of pads and helmet. He'd work hard physically for two hours of practice and I'd pick him up on the way home for dinner.

For a team of eleven- and twelve-year-olds, passing and catching the football are not priority practice items. So Chris spent most of his time blocking for running backs going inside or swinging around behind him. But, aware of Chris's developing glue-fingers, the savvy coach did put in a few basic pass plays, thinking they might be useful sometime. Even on his nonpractice days Chris and I would play in the street in front of our house. Line up. Check where the first down marker was. Wait for the signal. Go! No, no, make your cut sharply. Two steps before your turn you're leaning to the outside. That gives everything away. Sell your fake with your shoulders as hard as you make your real move. C'mon now, again. And again. Yes. Yes. That's more like it.

He got very good at snagging those passes along the sideline. Even without any opponents in our two-man practices, after making such a catch he remembered to run hard right down the sideline, the ball in the outside arm, the feet just inside the lines.

Then Spencer, my second son, became increasingly interested in football. Spencer wanted to play defense very much. Nothing would do but that he would try to defend against my passes to Chris. I was, of course, delighted with my younger boy's interest in football; he'd gotten a tiny pigskin in his crib, too. But being four years younger, Spencer was considerably smaller. I did not want him to become frustrated or discouraged because he could not keep up with someone older and larger. And as a brotherless only child, I was extremely uncomfortable with the idea of fierce competition between brothers. I loved competing against strangers, who don't matter because they are just stick figures obstructing victory. But brotherhood to me meant unconditionally and mutually belonging to someone of the same gender, like a two-member club, only stronger. The annoyance of each of my boys with the success of the other made me cringe inside. And I'd feel the need to try and defuse it.

But they both wanted to do it. And so I threw passes to Chris, and Spencer tried to bat each down or intercept it. Sometimes when Chris made a difficult catch, he would celebrate a bit too much for my taste. "Act like you've been there before," I said. And Spencer would simmer silently.

Sometimes the frustration of the other's success would boil over into anger, especially with Spence. "All right," I'd say. "Let's calm down a little. This is a game, remember, not World War Three." Then I'd show Spence how to read which way his opponent was likely to run or turn. Read the feet, not the shoulders. Minus to a plus.

The little guy got pretty good at defense. "I think you'd make a pretty good linebacker," I'd say. And Spence would say nothing, except, "Let's play some more."

At Chris's games, Spence usually wanted to run around

with other youngsters. But sometimes I'd get him seated and I'd pretend to be a linebacker reading the offense as it came up to the line of scrimmage. "Whaddya think it's gonna be?" I'd ask.

"Run!" said Spence.

"Remember, it's third and eight."

"Oh, pass."

And there would sail the ball. "Look," I said. "See, the linebacker thought it was a run. He took himself right out of the play. He left the whole middle wide open."

I enjoyed these moments immensely. I marked the game dates on my calendar. I'd get a minor wave of butterflies before each contest. Sitting in the stands, watching intently, I could make them evaporate after the first play or two. I didn't miss a game. When Chris's team was on offense, my eyes were riveted on him, No. 33. Every play held the potential for being the big one. Every play held the potential for learning something new, for reliving something old. That was on autumn Sundays.

On Saturdays came Spencer's contests in the old informal neighborhood league. Spencer wanted to be a running back in the worst way. They let him try. He was not fast or large. But he was very sturdy, very physical, and very unintimidatable, a football coach kind of word. And his obvious skills concerned playing defense. The coach made him a linebacker.

On the first seven plays of his first football game, Spencer made every tackle. After the seventh, the boy he had just put into the dust got up, slammed the ball back down, and pointed an accusing finger at Spencer. "He keeps tackling me," the child whined.

"Yes, son," said the referee. "That often happens in football. That's his job."

I was amazed at how different two sons from the same household could be at their ages. One was a methodical planner, had a fairly tidy room, and was a punctilious practice-goer who knew his plays and assignments and trotted off the field when the job of the offense was done. The other was a short dervish who not only didn't shun confrontations, he silently sought them. His dresser drawers seemed to spawn their own tornado systems. He wore whatever clothes were on top of the pile. He, too, was punctual for practice. Also very attentive and willing to try whatever the coach suggested. His system of playing had more madness than method. Wherever he ran, others fell down.

Neither one seemed intimidated by anyone or anything on the playing field. I was especially pleased by their businesslike approach and said so. It was exciting at each of their games, knowing one particular player but not knowing how he might react in the myriad circumstances that happen and not knowing how his action would affect the chemistry of his team, their team, and the game. There was joy many times and tension other times and the passing sadness of defeat. But everything was so unpredictable and vivid.

At a night game about mid-season Chris was doing his usual efficient blocking, which was anonymous except in the eagle eyes of his parent. On a nice end run to the left, he had leveled an opponent in the open field. The referee threw the flag for a clipping penalty. It was a close call. I watched Chris's reaction: nothing. He trotted back to the huddle, leaving the protesting to the coach. Good, very good.

Down near the goal, at about the ten, I saw Chris slide off his block and head into the end zone. Jeez, maybe they were finally going to throw him one. He faked to the outside, then ran across to the right, the surprised defender trailing. There went the ball through the bright lights, arcing up in his direction. Like so much about football, it was simultaneously full of tempting promise and ominous threat. I couldn't tell precisely from ground level, but he looked to be running out of field. The ball was heading out of bounds, properly; either he would catch it or no one would. Chris was reaching, stretching, keeping his body between the defender and the ball, dragging his feet to keep them inbounds, all as we had practiced. Then he was falling out of sight behind the other players.

I could see nothing. Dead silence. Nothing. Damn! Then I see a familiar arm jump above the crowd. The hand was holding the ball. Both the referee's arms shot up. Touchdown! Yes, oh, yes!

We relived that one many times. I probably enjoyed it as much as Chris did. In part, that was because, twenty years after I'd reluctantly shucked my pads, his success rekindled some inviting embers in my memory. He was traveling down a path that was fondly familiar. He'd have to negotiate the now-overgrown corners himself, but at least I had told him there would be corners. I had suggested some things in our personal practices and now I'd seen him assemble all the moves and execute the catch in his very own way. Practice pays. He could do it. He could do anything. And, someday, who knows, he'd pass on the same lessons through the same game to the next generation. There are probably only two people on earth who remember that play that night. But who cares? They're the two who matter. What began as a mere game became a living memory and, what's even better, it was shared.

"Remember how good this night feels," I suggested. "There will be others not so fine."

There were not many disappointments for that team. They were so well-organized and experienced, always stressing fundamentals first, always working in the newcomers with the veterans. There was one narrow, bitter loss to a suburb. "Well," I said, in the car later, "you've got to learn how to handle defeat, too." Which drew a funny look from Chris.

☐   ☐   ☐

There were bruises and frustrations in those seasons, of course, which is not unlike real life. There were rigorous exercises to perform to earn the right and the endurance to enjoy the game. I would help time his wind sprints. My

wife would arrange the proper diet to manage the weight
and energy levels. I couldn't wait for the games. When the
other team had the ball, I couldn't wait for us to get it.
When we had the ball, I couldn't wait for them to throw
to Chris, which they did more frequently.

Although my two sons were separated by a vast four
years, their mutual interest in and drive for the same game
seemed to bring them—all of us, really—together. Even
off the field. At one point Chris, like all his teammates,
had the assignment of selling raffle tickets to help finance
the team. If Chris sold twenty books of tickets, he could
have a leather team jacket for free. If not, he could buy
the jacket. In anticipation of not selling the requisite twenty
books, he had already saved $35 to buy the item of coveted
clothing with the embossed insignia and his number in the
team's colors. Although he thought nothing of blocking
opponents or running an intricate pass pattern in front of
a few hundred people holding their breath, the thought of
knocking on a stranger's door to peddle raffle tickets was
intimidating. As it was to me.

One day for company, Chris took Spencer along on his
neighborhood rounds. In the time that the offensive end
managed to sell four tickets, his little brother, the linebacker, sold a complete book. The seven-year-old, wearing
his numbered jersey and his wobbly toy football helmet,
didn't ask anyone *if* they wanted a ticket; he asked them
how many they wanted.

The two brothers made a deal. In return for selling more
than the twenty books, Spencer got his brother's $35 in
savings—so even at age seven, there could be money in
football. And Christopher got his free team jacket. For
Spence later, there was also a Most Valuable Player trophy,
a moment of joy and personal pride captured in a color
photograph where the youngster holds up his league's little
trophy and his party cup of hot chocolate at nearly equal
height.

And then came the run to the championship by Chris's

team. I should have expected the biggest personal play to come before the championship. These memorable times always seem to arrive at the most ordinary moments, as if they were waiting for a mental window when they're least expected and can have the most impact.

It was an away game, at night, cold, on a slightly soggy field. With the exception of that one narrow loss, Chris's team had rolled through the regular season methodically annihilating opponents by good-sized or oversized margins. They also had won the first two playoff games. This was the last qualifying encounter. A win here meant a trip to the championship. A loss meant the end of the season.

It was also their second game in barely four days. Because all I could do was watch, I was exhausted even before the kickoff. I have always been amazed at how well both boys handled what I regarded as intense pressure situations. They grow serious, markedly less jocular, quiet. But neither shows signs of the corrosive gnawing that for me sapped all pleasure out of wrestling. My nervousness usually emerges through yawns. Other parents in the stands could have thought I was very fatigued that night.

The game was painful to watch. The entire week had been one of the most distressing in Chris's life for some non-football-related reasons. I had told him that he need not play that night. But he insisted, so strong was his sense of commitment by then to his team. No one else had played his positon all year. But that night the whole team was flat. Lethargy reigned. They weren't blown away; their defense was just instinctively too good, even at its worst. But they weren't winning either. Three times the coach called a pass to Chris, his Mr. Reliable all season. Three times the ball hit Chris perfectly in the stomach. Three times he dropped it. Another father turned to me: "Nothing's going right for us tonight."

At the final two-minute warning, we were losing, 12–7.

The other team could already taste the sweetness of an upset victory. Our boys were being introduced to the gray of impending defeat. It is a scene etched in my mind forever. The runs up the middle by our battering fullback were going nowhere. The blocks weren't there and he was standing straight up. It was fourth down, ten yards to go on our own thirty-yard line. A minute forty-two seconds to go. Our last shot at winning. The entire season seemed to be on the line as Chris and the team broke from their huddle.

Any intent spectator there was expecting a pass. That's what last gasps are made of. I was watching the game like a linebacker, scanning the offensive lineup of my boy's team. I knew it was going to be a pass. And it was going to go to the outside so, if by some fluke, the ball was caught, the receiver could step out of bounds and stop the clock. More importantly, I knew the pass was going to Chris. I could tell by the formation and his enforced nonchalance. Oh, God, I thought. Every player has a nightmare; the nightmare of having the kind of game Chris was having. Every player has a daydream; the daydream of becoming the team's savior, catching a desperation pass or intercepting one, under pressure, that leads to victory. Now here they were, nightmare and daydream so close together they could merge at any second.

I had moved down near the sideline to pace back and forth. Now I stood frozen in one soggy spot. My feet were numb. My shoulders hunched, hands jammed into coat pockets, eyes riveted on my boy. He lined up ever so casually. He didn't even look at the defender facing him about eight yards away. The kid was giving Chris plenty of room and himself time to react. But Chris could use that strategy against the defender if he ran right at him quickly to eat up the kid's cushion, then sold him on a very good fake inside, and ducked to the outside as we had practiced so many times in the street. This time the curb was a painted chalk line in the mud.

The quarterback scanned the defense and stepped up to the center. He started calling the signals. The ball was snapped, too slowly by my mind. I knew exactly where my son was going. Chris charged right at the defender, who for a moment thought Chris was going to block him. He put up his hands. Chris moved his shoulders to the inside. The defender bought it. So, frankly did I. No, wait, he was angling back outside.

The defender recovered. But he was two steps behind. That would give Chris time before the hit to fully grasp the ball if it was on time and if it did get near him. Life was in slow-motion again. Chris was angling toward the sideline, his head slowly turned back over his left shoulder, his eyes groping for the ball in the bright lights. Good thing, too, because the ball was already en route.

It arced up higher and higher, a beautiful, bright brown against the dark sky. It kept coming and coming. C'mon, already. The defender will have too much time to catch up if Chris has to wait. Then the ball was falling, spinning, and falling slowly toward the sideline marker.

The ball got nearer and nearer. I could see the back of Chris's helmet tilting as his eyes looked the ball down. His hands were stretched out, little finger locking with little finger, elbows touching, like a basket. The ball settled in there so softly for such a violent game. Chris tucked the ball under his left arm. He caught it eleven yards from the line of scrimmage. First down!

Automatically, Chris turned quickly upfield. He ducked his head to avoid the flailing arm of the defender, who sailed by behind him. The kid was still going for the ball instead of giving Chris the catch and knocking him out of bounds to end the play. We still had nearly sixty yards to go and not much time.

Chris headed off down the sideline. The ball was under his outside arm; the defense would be going for it (Strip it! Strip it!) and if he did fumble, he wanted the ball to go out of bounds and remain in our possession. Chris stayed by the sideline; even if he was tackled, he could fall out, stop the clock, and save a precious timeout. The clock is running! The clock is running!

He ran fifteen more yards before another defender could arrive. That kid was desperate. He slammed Chris out of bounds. The clock stopped. First and ten on their forty-four. Still a very long way to go.

But our team's reaction was ecstatic. You'd have thought they just won the game. They were joyous, jumping up and down, screaming. The logjam of lethargy had been broken. Now they thought there really was a chance. Thought, hell. They knew it!

Our coach was screaming. He was not happy. Forget the celebrating. Take advantage of the other players' momentary disarray. Do not let them regroup and settle down. Strike quickly. We ran a power play right up the middle. The blocks were there and powerful. So was the old fullback, his legs churning, shoulders twisting, head down, eyes up. Twenty more yards. Yes, oh, yes!

Do it again. Yes. Five more. Now around end. Eight. The other side for two. First and goal on their nine. Timeout. Stop the clock. Nineteen seconds to go. No room for mistakes down here. Let the enemy stew in his chaos for a moment.

Take a deep breath. Line up. It's a pass! Another pass down here? Chris was running the same pattern. This time the defender would not be fooled. He was right on Chris's back as my son turned toward the sideline. But wait! No, the quarterback was handing it to the fullback again. It was a delayed draw up the middle. Through the line, the fullback cut into the area Chris's defender had just left vacant and thundered for the end zone. A frantic tackler hit him at the goal line. Too late!

Touchdown! TOUCHDOWN!

13–12.

Eight seconds to go.

Oh, my, yes. Oh, my, yes! How sweet this is! Whooee!

Parents hugging each other. Boys falling down in the grass. Laughing. Crying.

We kick the extra point: 14–12. Six seconds. Now somebody else needs a miracle. Now I need a new voice.

We kick off. Our defense was so pumped. They smother the runback. Not a chance for that kid. The gun went off. Victory City.

Well, I wasn't as exhausted as I thought. Neither were the boys, who disappeared into the locker room to hear the coach underline what they had just lived, to stoke their self-confidence and stress how important emotion and determination and continued concentration are under pressure. And now, boys, enjoy your hard work.

They blasted out of that doorway with joy as their ammo.

"Hey, guy," I said as he approached. We exchanged a hearty handshake that developed into an immense hug. Ten minutes later, in the quiet car, I told Chris how very proud I was of the way he hung in there, even when it seemed darkest, and kept on trying. I said that was good practice for life, too.

Chris said he had been a little nervous when they called his play in the huddle, when he lined up, and when he first found the ball already soaring toward him. What if I drop this one, too, he thought. "But then I remembered what you said about mistakes," he said.

"Oh, good," I said. I paused. "What did I say about mistakes?"

Chris looked puzzled a moment, as if fathers keep a mental transcript of every coachly quotation they hand out. "Well," he said, "about how if you keep thinking about past mistakes, they'll only cause new ones. So I put the drops out of my mind and just looked the ball into my hands like we do at home. And it worked, like you said."

Like my coaches said.

He leaned over against the car door then and went to sleep. I turned on the car heater and drove us home. The handoff had been made again.

□ □ □

After that scene, the victory in the championship game a few days later was almost anticlimactic, although I must say I got a real kick out of seeing his name and number go up on the stadium's huge scoreboard. Never having played on a championship team, I suggested he would savor the memory of that victory. "Those memories and that championship are things no one can ever take away from you," I said.

After we moved to Illinois, Chris played one more year of football, on the high school level, before his athletic interests took him into cross-country running for three years and then four years of college lacrosse.

As parents, we had busy weekends as conscientious spectators. In season, there were cross-country meets or ten-kilometer races. There, my wife, Connie, and I would exchange looks of anxiety as Chris pounded by after several miles. I cannot imagine a more grueling activity than long-distance running and wrestling. But every time he competed, Chris ran a better time. That made me proud, and I said so.

Both boys played baseball, both as catcher. I can picture them both shucking their face masks to block homeplate with their sturdy frames, taking the throw from center to place the tag, none too delicately, on some upstart base-runner trying for home. After one such dusty play, Spencer looked back at us through the backstop's screen. He smiled broadly. "Yes!" he said. "Contact baseball."

Our daughter, Emily, who was near Spencer's age, was totally uninterested in sports when she came from a Korean orphanage. She grew to relish some rather rugged football games with the boys, but seemed stunned when Connie, a youth league coach, signed her up for soccer. The initial games were hesitant, but Emily's blossoming self-confidence was visible off the field, too. And then came the crucial tie-game when Emily found herself near the enemy's goal, alone with the soccer ball, confronting a charging squad of defenders. Without thinking, she launched that round white missile on a swift arcing trajectory that drifted over the defenders to scoot by the startled goalie and win the game. The jubiliant gymnastics and congratulations by Emily's teammates were heady indeed. And to our delight, she has moved on to field hockey, basketball, and baseball. I warned her, too, about fingers on the bat when bunting.

Saturdays were devoted to Emily's soccer and Chris's running competitions. Sundays were for Spencer's football games. As he approached high school, the game grew more serious, as football does in the Midwest. The youth league was well organized and the coaches were fathers who had played the game, one or two of them professionally.

Spence was always assigned to play linebacker, which he took as a compliment. He was reckless at times, but the coaches saw his eagerness. In one game he charged right through a crowd of players watching a punt roll dead, seized the ball, and picked up maybe two yards. When the coach had recovered from his heart attack, he explained to his eager pupil that once he touched the ball, it was anybody's to take away. And the risk of losing possession at that time of that game on that spot on the field was really not worth the possible gain of six feet.

"Oh," said Spencer. "Okay."

One weekday a father who played linebacker in college showed Spence how to rush a kicker better. They practiced the move together the next couple of days. On Sunday, Spence actually tried the move. It worked. He blocked an extra point. I don't know who felt better—Spence, the other father, or me. But that wasn't the last time you saw that father take Spence aside for some extra tips.

Several fathers, most of us noncoaches, were usually hanging around the weekend practices, chatting, reminiscing about the previous week's game, assisting with a team drill or two, relishing our sons' dedication to and enjoyment of a vigorous sport we had once dedicated our once vibrant bodies to and enjoyed. The assumption of that shared interest felt good, a bond through the itch of dried grass sticking to sweaty backs. There was much talk, too, about the sheer fun of the game. There was silent satisfaction even in organizing the endless annual dinners where every coach was allowed to speak—and every parent was required to listen to—warm words about virtually every player, who each got a tiny trophy as take-home proof for Grandma and all to see that he had played on a real team that year.

A fair number of dads could be seen at our Sunday afternoon games wearing radio earphones to listen to favored professional teams play while watching their sons. What the boys saw, of course, although it didn't always register consciously for years to come, was that Dad deemed them more important than even a sacred Sunday off.

Some of the coaches were emotional and loud; some were quiet and distant. Some were attentive to every boy; some stroked only the stars. At the games, parents gathered on the sidelines, washing up and down the length of the field with the teams' movements. Between their playing stints, a few players would check in with their parents for accolades, although with approaching teendom most were beginning to sense the essential uncoolness of that.

Even though we were separated by the modest crowd or some yard markers, I never felt closer to my children than during these times. Each day they went off to school, of course, which is vital and all to learn society's approved lessons and packaged protocols. But so much of hands-on parenting is done on faith, like planting a fir tree. We believe it's right. We hope it's good. We probably won't be there to see the final product, to see all the lessons applied when that little seedling has grown into advanced adulthood.

But during these competitions, right now, that very afternoon, I could actually observe my children absorb teaching and hardships and apply real-life lessons in their own creative ways. If there was defeat, we could give a boost, hand out that sense of perspective that comes with the years and dims sad times. Trust me on this one, son, one day this won't seem so terrible. If there was victory, we could fan the flames of joy and underline the rewards of dedication. See what happens when you work hard and don't give up?

Maybe some parents were living or reliving childhood athletic fantasies or working out frustrations from the office or factory; I was merely trying to pass on the opportunity for him to live out his own dream versions. All right, I was also regularly urging him, too, yelling, "Strip it! Strip it!" I thought this was all great practice for the future and fun right now, which is more than you can say for, say, learning to balance a checkbook. Also, I enjoyed the unpredictable games myself, and I tried never to miss any, believing parental presence is such a powerful silent endorsement. These athletic experiences provided a fabric of fellowship, more even than I'd had with my own father, as well as a long string of memorable moments. There was the away-game when, the moment I saw the opposing quarterback's pass leave his hands, I knew it would end up in Spencer's arms. "Yes, oh, yes," I started to say. I had mentally extended the football's flight. I knew it would come down in my son's territory and I knew what his response would be. Sure enough, there it went. And sure enough, here came Spence. He'd measured the same mental arc. He knew the intended receiver could not get to the ball. So Spence had dropped his pass coverage and gone for the interception. The ball slammed right into his gut. He wrapped it up and ran straight ahead, bringing it back maybe fifteen yards. Then he got up and trotted to the sideline, as if he'd been there dozens of times.

One of my more satisfying memories had to do with someone else's son, appropriately named Andy, too. His parents were apparently not all that keen on his playing football. We never saw them at a practice or a game. They seemed to regard both as baby-sitting activities. Andy was a chubby fellow, twelve years old, not very athletic but eager to learn. Our coach played him regularly on kickoffs. It got the youngster in the game at a time when his inexperience would do the least damage.

We had one game against a city team whose very large members seemed able to defy gravity when they stepped onto the required pregame scales. They won the toss and elected to receive the kickoff. I happened to watch Andy on that play. He came barreling down the field like a kamikaze. He ran right into a blocker two or three feet taller. Suddenly, right in front of us, Andy was going backwards in the mud on his butt. The dads collectively winced.

"Are you okay, Andy?" they asked.

A dazed Andy did not answer as he made his way to the sidelines. Several fathers patted his back, more for surviving and getting back up than for any contribution his self-appointed suicide mission had made on the field.

I couldn't stand it anymore. Other people's kids are other people's kids. I was not the coach. But Andy's parents were not there. And our coach was too busy to see.

"Andy," I said, "come over here."

He followed.

"Okay, Andy. Now what's your job when we kick off?"

"To run down my lane and into that big guy."

"No, it's not."

"It's not?" He was puzzled, and hopeful, too.

"It's not. *His* job is to run into you. Your job is to cover your lane and then tackle the guy with the ball. Did this big guy have the ball?"

"No, sir."

"Have you ever seen him with the ball?"

"No, sir."

"Then don't waste time on him."

"But when I try to go around him, he gets in the way."

"That's his job. Each play is a collection of individual battles. Yours is very important. Now, if you get into a pushing match with him, then he wins because you're so busy with him you can't make the tackle. Understand?"

"Yes."

"And anyway, he's much bigger than you are. You're simply not going to go through him. Let's be honest, okay? You'll have to get around him some other way."

"But how *do* I get around him?"

"There's always another way. What do you say we try this. Next time we kick off to them, you come running down as fast as you can like you just did."

"Uh-huh."

"You come right at him."

"Uh-huh."

"But just before you hit, you step aside. Grab his shoulder pads—you're on defense so you can use your hands, right?"

"Uh-huh."

"Okay, you step aside like this. You grab him like this. And you throw him down like this. Use his own momentum against him. You're not strong enough to knock him back the other way; *I'm* probably not strong enough to knock him back the other way. But you're smart enough to outfox him. He's going forward. Help him go forward. Then he's out of your way. You can find the guy with the ball and nail him."

"Do you really think I can do that, Mr. Malcolm?"

"Of course you can. You can do anything when you use your head as well as your body."

Andy looked as if he wanted to believe me, but he was afraid to. I figured that I'd probably wasted my breath, although lavishing that brief time on Andy no doubt eased his embarrassment at being so totally dumped by the other kid.

It happened in the second half of that close game. We were kicking off after tying up the game. Here comes Andy barreling straight down the field. He obviously didn't remember a word I'd said. The big guy was bent over to level Andy again.

Then, just before they collided, Andy neatly stepped aside. He grabbed the back of the guy's shoulder pads and heaved. The big guy, braced for a devastating contact that didn't come, went flying on his own face into the mud. Andy sped, well, actually, he trundled on by. He'd covered his lane. Now, he could go hunting. And there just ahead was the ballcarrier. Andy ran right into him at the knees and pulled him down. The whistle blew. They'd gotten maybe six yards on the runback.

Andy had never gotten any cheers before that moment. But now our side erupted for him. Andy leapt up. He ran back to the sidelines, perhaps even faster than he had during the play. The smile was larger than his face mask. Yelling something, he ran right past all the smiling faces and out-stretched hands and straight down the sidelines to where I stood, applauding. "Mr. Malcolm!" he yelled. "I did it! I did it! Mr. Malcolm."

"Of course you did. You can do anything you want to, Andy. And don't you ever forget it."

Everyone on our sideline wanted to congratulate Andy. I hope he still carries that football memory around. Obviously, I do.

During these four years just before high school, Spencer's interest in wrestling began to bloom. There was a club and then a junior high team where he could use his few rudimentary moves and indulge himself in physical intimidation. Nothing seemed to phase him, not the anticipation of being out in front of a crowd alone, not the prospect of in-your-face and on-your-back competition, not even the prospect and occasional reality of losses. Merely the mention of a match could get my stomach churning very quickly.

A new assignment for me caused our family to move just before his freshman year, so he had to begin to construct his reputation for diligence all over, along with a whole network of friendships, which can come quickly on teams. Happily, the freshman football coach at his new school made him linebacker again. Sadly, my new job put me in

an office all day every day, even on the day of his first
freshman football game. So for the first time with either
boy I missed one.

I thought about him at kickoff time and early in the first
quarter. I imagined when they must be in the second
quarter. I imagined him at the half, sweaty, slightly tired,
sucking a section of orange with his wet hair matted on his
forehead, his shoulder pads bulging up behind his thick-
ening neck, his once-white jersey now muddy, but the No.
50 still visible. Probably, his eyeblack was running down
his cheeks. I could only guess when the game ended. But
I was desperate to know how it went.

About the time I figured he would be getting home, I
telephoned. He had just walked in the door, bursting with
happiness.

"Okay. Okay," he said, setting the scene. "We kick off
to start. They're on the twenty. Okay?"

"Okay."

"First down. Bishop—he's my new friend—he tackles
the back for a loss of two. Okay. Second and twelve."

"Okay."

"Second down they run up the middle and get back to
the twenty."

"Okay. Third down. Then what?"

"So I figure maybe a pass, you know, like the Arlington
game? I'm playing it a little wide. I'm watching the guard's
feet. Right away, I could tell he's pass-blocking. I see the
flanker stay in, so I figure it's a flat pass. I hide behind our
defensive end and about the time I figure the ball is coming,
I step out. There it is! I step in front. I grab it. Guess what,
Dad?"

"What? What?"

"Twenty-yard TD, baby!"

"Whooee! Spence, that's wonderful. Absolutely wonderful! Oh. Jeez. The first series in your first game at a new
school. Boy, some people can only dream of such things.
Congratulations!"

"Thanks. Thanks. It felt pretty good."

"I'll bet. Gee. Wow. I only wish I was there."

"Oh," my son said, "you were, Dad. You were."

□ □ □

That first year in the new school went well enough. From football he plunged into wrestling and earned a varsity letter as a freshman, accumulating a mediocre 8–4 record. In the spring, Spence tried lacrosse, which was new to him. He likened it to contact soccer. He thrived on the conditioning, the camaraderie, and the collisions. The second year Spence was a starter throughout the junior varsity football schedule, his eighth year at linebacker. Occasionally, with the cushion of a large lead the varsity coach would send in some J.V. players including Spence to gain experience. In the season's final game, Spencer got in for one inconsequential play, the last one of the year. Actually, it became the last two plays of the year. In his eagerness, Spence smashed into the opposing running back a split second after the whistle. Which drew a flag. Which led to one more play. Which led to our coach muttering, not for the first or last time, "I'll kill that fucking midget."

There was silent shock that first time, and nonplayers may still find some offense in such remarks. But as it was repeated over the next two years, the coach's hollow homicidal epithet began to draw more silent sideline smiles as a sign of rough affection for Spencer, who never heard the phrase directly during the ensuing scoldings. And the coach's silent actions, eventually naming Spence co-captain and defensive signal-caller and having him in the game virtually every play of his senior year, spoke louder than any mutterings.

That winter Spence had a markedly improved wrestling season. He took fifth place in the county tournament and fourth place in the state tournament. Which made him visibly hungry for more competition but not just head-on head-banging. In one wrestling match Spencer was dominated by the other boy, who was very good at a particular leg move. Spencer wasn't annihilated, but he was thoroughly controlled. Whatever he tried to do did not work.

Afterward, I went to commiserate and to ask him the familiar family questions that followed every defeat: Did you do your best and what did we learn from this experience? But I couldn't find Spence for ten minutes, until I spotted him emerging from the opposing team's locker room.

"I was just, uh, congratulating him," Spence said.

"Oh, yeah?"

"Yeah. And I asked him how he did that leg move."

"Oh, yeah?"

"Yeah. And he showed me." Spencer cackled then. "Last time that ever happens to me!"

Minus to a plus.

Then, in the spring-practice football scrimmage, I noticed a further inkling of athletic maturity. These spring encounters become part reward for two weeks of hard work and part advance indication of the coach's fall lineup.

It was a meaningless play on an overcast day. Spencer was at middle linebacker, his eyes scanning the opposing lineup through his face mask. At the snap everyone began moving to his left. So did Spencer, staying parallel to the line of scrimmage, keeping his options open while he helped string the play out. Eventually, going sideways, the offense would run out of playing field. It looked very much like an end run, the kind that, as recently as the previous autumn, would have found Spencer running pell-mell to get right in the middle.

But this time, as he began to roll to the left, Spence brought his head back to look to the right, too, checking for any tricks. Sure enough, there was the offensive end, slipping off of a fake block to run a delayed route across the territory they expected Spencer to have vacated.

Spence paused. He ducked down. The ball was on its

way. He leaped up. He snagged it. Interception. Very savvy.

That summer he attended a couple of college wrestling camps. There is nothing like experience in wrestling, going up against opponent after opponent, adding to the array of moves and countermoves he could do and anticipate. By the age of fifteen, of course, it was less cool to have parents around, so we had to settle for his secondhand reports.

By the time football practice began on the dried grass of those muggy early August mornings that presage scorchers by lunchtime, Spencer had drawn up his athletic targets for the coming year. The main goal was to do well in the county wrestling tournament come February. To that end, Spencer and Chris both had worked out intensively all summer. Even on vacation, they were out together in the heat, running along the rural roadsides up and down not-so-tiny hills, plunging into brisk mountain streams for momentary refreshment, moving large stones around, hauling dirt, and lifting weights.

Away at college, Chris had fallen in love with lacrosse. Due to the distance, I did not see every game. But each weekend I pictured him traveling across the Midwest to face off against other Big Ten schools. And I was eager for even fragmentary reports later. His lacrosse games that I did attend, though baffling to my eye in their complex and swift-flowing strategies, were hard-hitting dramas of determination and athleticism. My eyes were constantly glued on Chris's No. 44, which, not surprisingly, moved more like a man now than a boy. I liked the game. I liked watching my son play it. I liked his succeeding at it. I winced privately when he got hit hard. I whispered praise to him from the stands. Subtly, much of my enjoyment over the boys' sports had changed from their doing some things I had done a generation before, to their doing some things I never could do.

Both boys had very good men for their athletic coaches

in each sport, men who devote countless hours of their free time to spotting and developing the athletic and mental skills in each class of upcoming young men and the rare combinations of both. These pros could deal with the moves, the countermoves, and the strategies. With Christopher largely off on his own now as a hustling team captain, I appointed myself psyche coach to Spencer. I said, as my own coaches had suggested many years before in their own ways, that the February wrestling tournament would take care of itself if we took the intervening months of academic and athletic work one step at a time. We could keep February vaguely in mind but meantime focus on each immediate challenge. I said he could not expect to switch on championship intensity on February 1. It would have to start now, today, with his summer training. He pursued his running and weights with a vengeance.

The morning of each game or match I gave him a note of encouragement or urging. He took to slipping each one into his left sock, where they were destined to dissolve in sweat. I don't know if these slips of paper accomplished anything for the game. But they sure made me feel a part of the action.

Then, after each wrestling match, we would find each other's face in the crowd and we would each hold up one forefinger signifying the completion of one more step. A win was great, but just one step. A loss was too bad, but just one loss.

In football, there were a few losses. The football coach told a newspaper reporter he had been worried about Spencer's size and speed previously, but those concerns were soon outweighed by the player's determination. Spencer felt some moments of genuine anger (maybe even synthetic hate) toward his athletic bosses, and vice versa, I assume. Emotions get so magnified, so deliciously, in football. But when the coaches told Spence to shadow an opposing back throughout a game, he did. When the coaches told Spence that when a hole opened up this way, he should run into it without thinking, he did. Step up, they yelled. So he stepped up. Ka-blam! Spencer would get smashed by some blocker or running back coming through.

But Spence had been able to mess up their plans, to buy time for his teammates, and sometimes, despite the impact we could hear up in the stands, he'd also make those tackles. He wouldn't just fill the hole with his body; he'd go right on charging through, trying to use his own momentum for his own protection. One time one huge, six-foot back got as far as the line of scrimmage. Spence hit him so hard, he stood up straight. He fell backward. Loss of two that time.

As his brother before him, Spence didn't stand around jawing at the momentarily vanquished opponent. I had suggested from experience that that would lead to an inevitable lapse in his concentration. In football, as in life, the bad guys have a way of winning for a while. But in football, as in life sometimes, the tables have a regular way of turning around real quick, leaving the blowhards with words splattered all over the front of their shirts. Just let your actions do the talking on the field. And off.

Spence intercepted another pass because he read the young quarterback's eyes, and he ran the ball back over thirty yards. Look at those legs go! In the same game amid the arm-swinging, knee-pumping melee at the line of scrimmage, Spencer took the ball away from a passing offensive back. "Spence is having quite a day," another father said to our concentrating group of football fathers way up in the stands. Everyone agreed. I glowed privately.

The local newspaper had a photo of No. 50 rising from the pack holding the ball high in the air triumphantly. Spencer's mother was uncomfortable, suggesting that was showboating. "No, Mom, honest, I wasn't," he said. "I just wanted to show Dad I finally stripped it."

Our coach, meanwhile, continued his fondness for choosing a wrestler to play center, one of the most challenging physical and mental positions. He didn't care if Spence or his previous center were among the smallest boys on the football field. "Wrestlers aren't intimidated," said the football coach. "And they know leverage." Minus to a plus. By the end of his junior football season, Spence was starting center and linebacker. He was picked for an all-suburban team. "Spencer Malcolm," the paper quoted his coach, "is a heat-seeking missile." It was but one step, to be sure, but it felt very good, at least up in the stands.

In December, Spence began the wrestling season, a methodical march through two dozen opponents one step at a time. It required endless hours of practice, even more conditioning than football, use of different muscles, physical and mental, and an intensity that was somewhat frightening. In these times his grades actually improved. For me, those ten weeks of wrestling were difficult. Knowing little about modern scholastic wrestling and not having exactly excelled at old-time scholastic wrestling, I was unprepared to sit in the stands for long hours of waiting punctuated by brief, but endless moments of terror as my son walked out on the mat to confront someone else's sweating son of equal weight. My stomach felt frozen. My limbs overflowed with nervous energy. My mind was numb. I yawned a great deal.

I made it to almost every match, but I did not look forward to those days, so full of nervous echoes were they for me. Like he did matside, I had a semicomforting routine before each contest in all those nondescript gymnasiums where good acoustics are as common as clean socks. My meaningless rituals provided a sense of control over uncontrollable events, if I just did everything exactly the same as I did for the last victory. The gods were, after all, always watching closely. Of course, I was wearing a lucky shirt and the same shoes and pants as I had worn the last time. I sat the same way that I remembered sitting at the same times leading up to previous matches. I put the videocamera in the same place beneath my legs, setting the dials the same and uncapping the lens at the same stage before each match. I even used the same battery. I yelled the same thing as he walked onto the mat. I mumbled the same simple prayer to myself. And I ran the video-recording equipment to keep my hands and mind busy. It only mattered in my mind, of course, which, come to think of it, is the only place it should have mattered.

Spencer knew what he was doing; I didn't. Unlike football, a large lead in wrestling points is meaningless, so quickly can a determined opponent's one move turn the tables and lead to a pin. So there was no relaxing for me during any match until the time expired and the referee raised his hand in victory. "Yessir!" I'd yell in relief as well as exultation. And in a moment our eyes were meeting across the gym as we each raised one forefinger.

These were wonderful parental experiences. They were not pleasant personal experiences. His competing, his intensity and focus, his skills spawned bounteous pride and were wonders to behold. My own feelings while witnessing them were not. As the years had passed, I had grown calmer at these times. I still think that some pharmaceutical giant could assure its financial future by inventing a mild over-the-counter sedative for parents of scholastic athletes—"Watch your child compete, and this time enjoy it, with ParentCalm, the antianxiety pill for adults." But I could never not be there.

"Dad," Spencer said during a break at one tournament, "you looked really nervous before the last match."

"Uh-huh," I said. "That makes real good sense because I was. I'm sorry if it bothers you."

"No, hey," he said, "that's okay. But if it's any help, I'm having a great time out there."

"Thanks, son."

Of course, my son did not disappoint me or himself. He was always focused, even on his off-days. He knew what he wanted. He knew what it would take. He was prepared to invest the physical and emotional effort. I was along for the ride, the familiar presence with the occasional supportive reminder, keeping the highs from getting too high and the lows from too low. Although at times I had to convince myself first. Do as I say, not as I do.

It worked. Spence went into the county tournament with seventeen victories, won one at a time, and no defeats.

"Dad," he said, "I have to say I'm really nervous for this one."

"Well, that's natural," I said. "So are your opponents. If you weren't a little on edge, I'd be worried. You can do it. You know you can. I know you can. Use the nervousness to fuel your determination, not corrode your confidence. And have fun. This isn't World War Three, you know."

Two days later he came out of that gymnasium with twenty victories and no defeats, carrying the beribboned medal of a new county champion.

"This is great," he said.

"Enjoy it," I said. "You earned it."

A week later, Spencer placed fifth in the state tournament, a disappointment. Back in youth league football, Spencer and his buddies had gotten themselves pumped at school one day for that evening's game. But they had played a messy game and lost decisively. I'd asked him then what the lesson of that loss was. He knew it instantly. "Don't get pumped at four," he said, "when the game isn't 'til seven."

Now we had to work on some emotional endurance. "Well," I told Spence, "you reached your goal for this February. Now you've got something to work for next year." I thought, frankly, that seemed like a very long road to travel, until I remembered what a nurseryman had replied one time when I made a similar remark about how many years it took trees to mature: "You're planning on being here then anyway, aren't you?"

In silent reply, Spencer reluctantly dropped lacrosse to devote the entire spring's free time to being an itinerant wrestler, continuing his own training and wandering around the region, entering tournament after tournament to hone his skills against the unpredictable moves of unfamiliar opponents. In the summer, there was more time at wrestling camps and daily sessions on our weight set.

The fall began with his appointment as football co-captain, an honor that I recorded with pregame snapshots taken from such a distance that his No. 50 was barely visible.

The late-summer football training was, as usual, onerous. Spence kept telling himself, "*This* is the last time. *This* is the last time." At the same time I was thinking, "This is the *last* time. This is the *last* time." There was more thinking this football season, too. As center, Spence had to be herding the offense into the huddle, sometimes before the pile from the previous play was dismantled. On defense he was getting the signals from the sidelines, passing them on in that huddle, barking warnings just before the play started, making his own readings as it unfolded. Sitting in the stands, watching the action up close with one eye through the telescopic viewfinder of my video camera, I tried to play right along with him. I hardly ever followed just the ball. If Spencer was near the ball, I'd get the ball. If not, I didn't. This game was between us. Near the end of the first quarter came my familiar urge to yell, "Strip the ball! Strip it!"

I especially enjoyed our kickoffs. First of all, they usually meant we had just scored. But mainly it was to watch No. 50 rush down the field. His job in these dramatic field-long encounters was to break up the blocking wedge forming as protection in front of the ballcarrier. If Spence could make the tackle, too, that was fine. But his main job was to fracture the assembling armor of other players. It was an incongruous assignment, sending probably the lightest player on the field to mess up two or three bulky behemoths. Spence took great pride in this. I took great pride in his pride, especially when I heard strangers conversing behind me. "Look at that 50 kid!" I imagined Spencer imagining such remarks. So I passed them on afterward, as my contribution toward rewarding excellence.

For once, it happened when I was ready.

All through my childhood, I had portaged a fielder's glove to countless professional baseball games, ever hopeful despite the statistics of a foul ball flying my way. The closest one ever came was several seats away behind third base at Cleveland's stadium. I rushed over. The sacred, scuffed orb was laying there, tantalizingly, momentarily, in the shadows on the rough cement amid the shattered peanut shells and half-crunched beer cups. So near. I reached for it. A man came crashing in from the side and stole it. The feelings I had at that moment have remained the most powerful argument I know against allowing eleven-year-olds to carry firearms.

For those delectable moments of sports glory in my children's lives, I had always forgotten the camera or decided against bringing it for fear of rain or I got so excited when the dramatic catch came that I forgot to shoot the picture or jerked the camera so everything was out of focus, except our memory.

Now, in this my second son's final football season, I had finally learned my lesson. I was going to videotape every moment of every contest. It was a bitter cold Friday night, an away-game. I wore one regular glove and one of those with holes at the end of each finger, so I could run the camera.

Fourth quarter. We're ahead 19–12. Spencer had intercepted a goal line pass that could have tied the game up. Now, thanks to some sharp passing, the enemy is driving again toward our territory. First and ten on their own forty-yard line. They send a flanker way out to the left side toward me. Spencer edges out slightly but stays close to the middle. He's got a defensive back to come up quickly for help, if necessary.

For some reason, looking through the viewfinder, this time I back off the close-up of Spence to take in most of the field. Spence on the lens's left side, crouched, watching feet and the ball. This flanker kid stands way out in the open, all loose and eager. The kid isn't looking downfield, planning his fakes for there. He's watching the quarterback closely, too closely. Which means he's a savvy faker, too savvy for high school, or they'll probably snap the ball and just fire it out to the flanker as fast as possible in hopes that Spencer is too slow or the defensive back will miss the tackle. And they'll get a long gain or a quick TD. There's not much time left for them. And the clock is running.

The ball is snapped. The quarterback is turning to his left. Spencer is off like a shot toward the flanker. There's no running back on the quarterback's left, so there are only two reasons why he'd turn that way. Either he's going to run around left end or he's going to throw it to that flanker.

Spence guesses the throw. He's right. The quarterback zips the ball out there nicely. The flanker looks it into his hands. He turns upfield. He covers maybe two or three yards before Spence slams into him. He hits him up high, which is a little dangerous since, if the kid is big, one good shoulder shake and Spencer is shucked. But this kid isn't big. Spence has him by the waist. The defensive back arrives and hits him low. The flanker is struggling. He's leaning, but he isn't down yet.

This all happens within a few instants. I'm zooming in on these three struggling youths, thinking it would be a perfect time for our blessed boys in blue to steal the ball from these brazen bullies in black. Losing possession would likely crush the enemy's spirit. And, I can't see through the lens, but I'll bet there's no one between this forty-two-yard line and the goal line. Either goal line.

Strip it, Spence! Strip it!

He's got his back to me. But his arms are flailing. Good. Good. The struggling flanker is still not down. The referee is right there. He has the whistle in his mouth. But he's backing away now. As if he sees something about to happen. Yes? Yes. Yes! Now Spence is backing away. Now the flanker is flailing. And falling.

I can't see the ball. No one up here can. I know Spence has got it. He would. Run, guy, run. He runs. Oh, how he runs. Now our sideline realizes what's happening. The flanker has lost the ball. Which means Spencer has found it! Everyone jumps up and down, including the coach. Look at that midget go! Now Spence has a blocking escort. He doesn't need him. But it looks great. Spence is still running, knowing six succulent points await just a little ways away. But now Spence is falling, in the grass, in the end zone, beneath his boisterous buddies. Oh, yes, oh, yes, oh, yes! He did it. Just like we talked. The opportunity came. You made your own luck. You did it!

And I got every move of his memorable miracle on tape. What a team we are. All right, so the pictures get a little bumpy after he goes down in the end zone. And the sound-track is full of a grown man losing his voice. But I caught the important part.

Our sideline is going berserk. It's 25–12 now, soon to be 26–12. They are finished. Finito. In the remaining few minutes they will get zero points. Nada. De rien.

According to high school etiquette, our coach sends in the subs, to avoid rubbing the loss in. He waits one more play to replace Spence. That way the kid gets his own ovation from our frozen hands.

That season turned out to be fair. We won more than we lost. The boys had their share of thrills and joys as interest paid on their investments of emotion and sweat. They had their share of disappointments, as practice for off-field life, later. The coaches had their share of fuming frustrations because this game is their later life. The parents got to see and record it all and to remember select parts, which sometimes actually match what shows up on tape. And I got to share some more with Spence.

It's the little memories that make up that fond fabric of thoughts. Like the close game where the other team's running back got around our left defensive end and seemed headed for six points sixty yards away. I'm watching with one eye again through the narrow mind of the camera's lens. I'm following this guy as he streaks down the chalk marks of our sideline. There is no one between him and the goal line. I'm regretting his success. Our stands are silent. Their stands are erupting. And I'm thinking, it's not Spence's responsibility, but if he started hustling from the other side of the field as soon as he realized where the ball was going, and if he took the correct running angle, and if he ran as hard as those little legs will go, my boy should be coming into the picture right . . . about . . . now. And right then, from the side of the picture comes No. 50. Our last hope to prevent six points.

Forget the tackle, I'm thinking. Stretch out. Leap low, right in front of the runner's knees. The back has nowhere else to go. Spence, knock the kid's legs out of bounds. And stop the clock while you're at it.

Suddenly, there's my boy stretching out. He leaps low, right in front of the runner's knees. The back has nowhere else to go. Spence knocks the kid's legs out of bounds. And stops the clock while he's at it.

Spence bounces up quickly then. His teammates pat his back. The running back is slower. He's lost his breath. Spence trots back out on the field, all businesslike. Let them worry about their points and plays. You take care of yours.

What looked like an overpowering outburst for the other team has become just a nice gain. What looked like disaster for us has become a mark of determination. A man turns to me in the stands. "If we pull this win off," he says, "that play will be the turning point."

We don't. Our offense stalls again. The opposing team takes care of earning its points and executing its plays. We don't. But that one brief little play sticks in my memory. As he trots back out to call the next defensive signals, Spence doesn't look up in the stands. He doesn't have to. Even all those rows apart, we are very close. You can tell because neither one of us thinks a thing about it.

198 □   ANDREW H. MALCOLM

□   □   □

Last games are tough games. They should never end. When
I was a youngster, I was an eager attendee at the birthday
parties of pals, meaning mostly boys. In part, this was due
to the ubiquitous chocolate cake and ice cream, which only
came in that combination at other people's houses. But also
in part, I loved these affairs because they presented yet one
more chance to win a game of musical chairs, no, to capture
it. In my circle of friends, musical chairs was not a dainty
dance around a dwindling circle of antique, crochet-covered
dining room chairs with little boys in best clothes gently
bumping into each other. In our games no one ever said,
"Excuse me."

   In fact, musical chairs was my first contact sport. If a dad
was running the birthday party games, we rowdies loved
tackling each other as soon as the music stopped. Sometimes even before. You know, you need to have the right
angle at every possible moment. We'd trip each other and
push and claw our way up and over assorted squirming
bodies to the sacred prize, the lone remaining vinyl-covered
cushion of a metal kitchen chair. In these games in those
days, there was no prize but victory, just the sweet satisfaction of sitting there, disheveled king of the mountain for
a magic moment. After the food and the initial round of
games, we might scurry outside for more competition or,
in winter, be driven to the Saturday matinee, so we wouldn't
miss an episode of the latest Don Winslow of the Coast
Guard serial.

   Those were the days before movies came into the home
on TV, on cable, or on rental cassettes. So they seemed
very special. Last week Don, who was the good guy because
his uniform was all white, had been trapped in his crashing
plane. That Saturday, of course, he would somehow extri-
cate himself, clamber into his hidden but very fast speed-
boat, and rush back to his secret hideaway that no evildoers
could find—although one came close one Saturday—be-

cause it was behind a huge waterfall that Don could turn off with a switch on his boat dashboard. Oh, there was also a regular movie along with the Don Winslow serial, probably a Western with Gene Autry. Gene was better than Roy Rogers because Gene's horse, Champion, was smarter than Trigger and didn't wear so much chrome and Gene didn't always have a girl named Dale hanging around. Also, thanks to my Saturday matinee quarters, Gene eventually got into baseball—well, actually owning a baseball team—and Roy got into roast beef sandwiches, which are good and all but sandwiches don't win the World Series. Of course, neither do the California Angels. But who knew about all that at age six?

After the main movie we would return to the birthday boy's house to work off the candy bars by resuming our musical chairs competition, which is a lot like life if you think about the initially happy crowd dwindling when the music is interrupted and the players fall by the wayside as the game winds down.

Now, I was glad to have parents. Everyone should have them. But mine were Canadian, which meant they were very concerned about what people might say if they arrived to reclaim their only son twenty-four seconds after the party's official termination time. There is nothing Canadians can do to cure this rampant thoughtfulness. It's genetic, something about survival on the tundra during unexpected blizzards. So my punctual parents would be the first to arrive, even in summer. They would come together, Mom to put a civilized, social face on everything and Dad for ominous enforcement should their party boy be inclined to resist being reclaimed. Now, why ever would they anticipate such a thing?

Mom would begin silently tucking my best shirt back in, lest someone on the street see a six-year-old with his best clothes in disarray. We would stand near the door while Mom pulled my pants up straight and then went to work on my face, removing the chocolate smudges in the general mouth area, although the elbow vicinity was often involved, too. "How did you get chocolate on your elbow?" is one of those questions—like ancient Inca landing pads—that have no answers but are nonetheless always taught in Motherhood School. The inevitable chocolate tracks had to be removed for reasons that were so obvious to mothers they never needed explanation. Mom used tissues that seemed to grow inside her purse. Of course, I knew that was ridiculous; tissues come in boxes where they are meticulously folded together by immigrant Irish elves who must climb out before the boxes leave the factory because I never found any little people the times I removed every folded tissue one at a time. Coming upon a tissue box restuffed with 198 new but not so neatly refolded paper tissues would prompt my mother to sigh. "I told you there are no elves in the Kleenex box!"

During these doorway cleanups I would express the desire to stay at the party a while longer. My parents would demur, smiling. I would plead. They would demur, still smiling and suggesting that the birthday boy's mommy and daddy probably had other things to do.

Who cared about them? They weren't in the way, as long as one of them ran the phonograph for tackle musical chairs. I didn't hear them complaining about doubling the length of their boy's birthday revelries.

I would suggest that my parents return in, say, an hour. No, make it two. They would demur, not smiling. "Now, Andrew," they would say, which was the warning signal. Using a formal name was the red light on the dashboard of youth. "Now, Andrew, all good things must come to an end."

"Why?"

I never did get an answer. My parents and his parents would just exchange phony smiles. And suddenly I'm outta there. Blame it on all that sugar.

But good things, and good games, do seem to come to an end always. And after all those lush and seemingly endless good times and after all that forgetting of the less good times, there suddenly looms the last one. And instead of just enjoying it, I spend much of the last one thinking, Darn, this is the last one.

The previous spring I had been sitting at this same desk writing another book on a Thursday morning. The coming weekend was to be Chris's last university lacrosse competition. I know it's natural that our youngsters grow up from playing catch with the Mickey Mouse ball on the living room carpet to T-ball to Little League to Pony League to high school to college, when reports of all these doings first start to trickle in secondhand via collect phone calls. Secondhand sucks. I prefer the colorized, real-life versions. Intellectually, I knew about the inevitability of all this. But emotionally accepting the graduation of such a team member is something quite different. I had avoided it quite successfully for both boys.

"You know," I said turning to my wife, "I really wish I'd made plans to go see Chris play one last time this weekend."

"So why don't you?" she said.

Yeah, why don't I? So I did. Unannounced. I arose way before dawn and took a last-minute flight halfway across the country. I dashed across the world's busiest airport. I took any car rental they had and raced down a pair of expressways and a maze of local streets to the playing field. And there, after eight hours of traveling, I ran up to the sidelines, breathless, ten seconds before Chris ducked around a defender and whipped the hard rubber ball into the enemy's goal.

"Yes!" I yelled. "Way to go, Chris!"

No. 44 froze in mid-step. He looked over. His jaw dropped. He smiled. After the game, we embraced emotionally and had our pictures taken because the damned videocam wasn't working properly. He had given me an official game jersey and I proudly wore it all day. No. 44, too. It was great to watch him again in those games. I felt

so alive to see him so alive, so determined, so ferocious at
times, so content competing. I had thought, sadly and mis-
takenly, that that link had been outgrown like an old uniform. It had not. It had just taken on a new form. Another
priceless lesson from a game.

Now, a few months later, there we were, my wife and I,
standing on the sidelines at Spencer's last home football
game awaiting the special ceremony for seniors and their
parents. They called out his name and number. He came
charging out of the end zone in his freshly laundered blue-
and-white uniform with the nearly clean knees, past the
noisy band, down the row of leaping cheerleaders, and up
to us. He gave his mother a rose. She gave him a good-
luck charm. We exchanged hugs.

"Go get 'em, champ," I said.

"Thanks, Dad," he said.

And then he was gone, out onto that playing field and
all the playing fields to come.

□ □ □

There was much more competition to come, of course. The
wrestling season. The tension. The work. The dedication.
The hard work. The hopes. The frustrations. The pranks.
The dreams of soaring. The fears of falling. The headiness
and uncertainty of being recruited by colleges. The season
was complicated, physically and emotionally, by a serious
bout with mono. But he pursued the recovery with the same
patience and determination as he did his opponents on the
mat.

This makes everything sound too easy, but he repeated
as county champion. He did become state champ, too, the
first in his school's history. And he placed sixth in the region. "You know," he admitted to me in the car on the
long drive home, "I didn't know if I could do it."

I had been a nervous wreck for three succeeding weekends of travel and competition, being extremely busy with
the camera, yawning a good deal, and sitting in silent awe

of a former little guy who was creating the most magnificent set of memories of his own. "Of course you didn't know," I said calmly. "But now you do."

"Yeah," he said. He leaned over against the car door then and went to sleep.

□ □ □

He's gone off to university now, too, of course. Our reports of his distant Division I NCAA competitions come largely secondhand, which reduces the required dosage of antacids but turns them into black-and-white experiences. As with Chris, I'm more of a spectator in absentia, which is natural, I guess. I'm still the father, of course. But there is a whole string of coaches whose full-time job it is to teach and chide. My boy is doing things I never even dreamed of when I took my mental flights through those white, puffy clouds that slipped through my fingers.

The sports links with my sons remain, naturally, although they are different. We have the shared memories of tense times and joyous ones, of ersatz family games in the street where the brothers both reached for the ball. Football and sports hang like a backdrop in our family life. If a Browns game is on TV and one of their receivers makes a spectacular catch, I'm not surprised when the phone rings moments later and, without any transcontinental greeting, Chris's voice says, "Did you see that?"

I can bring a smile to their faces, too, simply by chanting urgently, "The clock is running! The clock is running!" And during their pickup games with friends, I've heard both boys provide their own running narrations.

There is, however, a new wrinkle in all this. I have a new son, Keddy. He's barely three years old, big for his age, but not given to easy intimidation even at the height of barely forty-two inches. He runs into things or people and falls down but does not cry. He wrestles with Spence. He loved to run around wearing his brother's huge football helmet, which wobbled all around his little blond head.

Keddy got a mini-football in his crib and now he wants to play knockdown games. He's got low-fives and high-fives down pat. And he loves the Strip It! game, although playfully knocking things out of the hands of preschool pals is not appreciated by his teacher, who never played linebacker.

We watch baseball together, Keddy and I. Even car races. When a football punter lofts the ball high into the stadium lights, Keddy asks, "What's the ball do-ning?" When the teams line up and the quarterback calls signals, Keddy orders, "Go!" And when the teams on TV respond perfectly to his command, there are giggles of glee. When someone, anyone, is running, Keddy provides succinct commentary: "Running. Running. Running." When the runner is tackled, he issues the same comment, "Oh! Too bad."

I love it.

I also loved it when, on the spur of the moment during a long springtime weekend back in my hometown, we looked up a friend who works at Cleveland Stadium. "Would Keddy like to see the field?" he asked. Does ice cream melt? If Keddy didn't know, his father did.

We jumped down on to the dirt track by the third-base dugout, right below where Dad and I used to sit. Keddy wasn't sure what was going on. But we ran across the lush grass. We strode up to the plate. We looked down the third-base line. We looked down the first-base line. We stared down the invisible pitcher. And then, in that magnificent empty ediface where 82,000 have gathered to admire athletic endeavors, in front of three cheering fans, without even a bat, Keddy Colton Malcolm hit his first grand-slam homer.

First, he ran to first; okay, first he headed for third. But he made it to first, where Vic Wertz used to guard the bag so closely. With his new Indians hat only slightly askew, Keddy turned for second, spanning that red dirt that Bobby Avila and his quick feet patroled with such admirable nervous energy. Keddy zipped, then, past the shortstop position, George Strickland's former patch of dirt, and rounded third, where big Al Rosen covered the bag. Just before he got home, Keddy stopped.

The fans were screaming. The clock was running. "Like this," I said, jumping on homeplate with both feet. He watched my face and did nothing.

"No," I said. "Watch my feet."

His head went down. I jumped on homeplate. With both feet. I stepped back.

"Go on."

He smiled.

He wound himself up. He jumped on homeplate. With both feet.

The stadium went wild. Keddy did it! Keddy did it! The home team won.

There were congratulations all around and very professional high-fives, which are actually high-fives for Keddy and low-fives for Daddy. It was just one game. But becoming a hero can be exhausting, even in dreams. Our two-man home team headed home. As we worked our way up the cratered old cement steps, I saw it sitting there in the dark shadows beneath a row of seats. It seemed unbelievable after all this time. And perfectly timed, since I was not ready; I had not brought my glove. But there it was just below where I had so often watched so long, ready in vain. It was just sitting there, round and scuffed. Waiting for the next dreamer.

"Oh, Keddy. Look!" I said. "What's that?"

He walked over as if it might bite. He stuck his chubby little hand down into the darkness, then picked something up with great excitement. He turned around, all aglow. "Ball!" said my little son.

Minus to a plus.